What You Can Say...

When You Don't Know What to Say

What You Can Say...

When You Don't Know What to Say

Lauren Briggs

HARVEST HOUSE PUBLISHERS
Eugene, Oregon 97402

WHAT YOU CAN SAY...
WHEN YOU DON'T KNOW WHAT TO SAY

Copyright © 1985 by Harvest House Publishers
Eugene, Oregon 97402

Library of Congress Catalog Card Number 85-060125
ISBN 0-89081-465-1

Printed in the United States of America.

*To every person whose life has been
touched by tragedy and especially those who
have lovingly shared their hurts and
victories teaching me how to be a
more effective comforter*

AND

*To my husband, Randy, and my sons,
Randy, Jr. and Jonathan, who are a source
of joy in my life.*

FOREWORD

I remember so clearly those days when, one after another, I held in my arms two sons who were born with irreversible brain damage. I had been a well-known civic and church leader in the community, and my home had always been bustling with activity. Once friends found that I had a second baby with the same symptoms, they stopped coming to see me. From days of joy and laughter, I went to months of loneliness and depression. I didn't know why the people who loved me in fair weather forgot me in the rain.

As I look back I realize it wasn't that people didn't like me anymore; it was that they DIDN'T KNOW WHAT TO SAY. What do you say to a grieving mother? What do you say to a friend in need? No one seems to know, so it's easier to stay away.

If there is one thing a mother does not want, it is for any of her children to go through the same hurts she has suffered, so when my son-in-law called to say Lauren had lost her baby girl in her fifth month of pregnancy, my heart was truly broken. How could this happen again? Why did my daughter have to face an infant death?

Again, few people knew what to say. As Lauren worked through her grief, she made note of the helpful and hurtful things friends did and began to share these thoughts with others. As she spoke before 700 women at the Arizona Women's retreat, I observed her compassionate spirit and sincerity. Those in the audience hung on her every word as she shared practical suggestions of how they can effectively reach out and comfort their hurting friends. When the evaluations were tallied, she came out as the speaker who had most closely met the needs of the women.

We don't know what to say, but Lauren does and she's willing to tell us.

Florence Littauer

Contents

1

I Don't Know What to Say

Picture yourself sitting on the couch watching TV when a news brief flashes on the screen. "There's been a plane crash on Catalina Island and all passengers aboard were killed."

I hate small planes, you think. *They never have seemed safe to me.* But the next day you receive the shocking news. Two people aboard that plane were your parents' close friends.

Picture yourself standing in the kitchen one bright sunny morning when the phone rings. It's your church's prayer chain. "Please pray for four students of Arrowhead Christian Academy who were seriously injured in a head-on collision."

You hang up the phone and pray for their recovery. *Were they driving carefully?* you wonder. The incident fades from your mind until hours later when you

11

learn that one of the students you've been praying for was the son of a family friend—a boy you'd babysat when you were younger. He died in that crash.

On another day imagine you're waiting in the maternity ward for a friend who's about to deliver her second child. You think about how excited she and her husband are and what a good mother she is. Nothing is more important to your friend than motherhood.

You're getting impatient. With the contractions about three minutes apart, it should be soon.

The next moment, you look up and see your friend's husband coming through the doorway from the delivery suite. He stands before you, his arms hanging helplessly at his sides. His words are anguished. "Our baby has died."

What to Say

All these experiences happened to me. Each time, I felt overwhelmed with grief. What could I say to the family of those two friends who'd been buried in the wreckage of a plane? To the mom and dad who'd lost their young son Nathan in a car crash? What could I possibly say to ease the pain of parents who had been anticipating joy and were facing tragedy instead?

Have you had this problem? Have you wanted to comfort a friend and yet not known how to express your feelings? As I sorted through the horror and shock of each tragedy, I realized I simply didn't know how to comfort the family. I had to deal with my own feelings of loss and questions before I could reach out and minister to anyone else.

After Nathan's death, I was so upset that I couldn't call the family so I decided to look for a card.

Quickly, I went to the store. At a rack labelled "Sympathy," I read one card after another. None of them, however, came close to expressing the intensity of this family's loss or my deep compassion for them. They were filled with empty platitudes and hopeful euphemisms.

These messages wouldn't comfort my friends; they might even offend them with references to "the flowers of the future" and "a better home beyond."

Finally, I stopped searching for a sympathy card that would express my own sorrow and concern and looked for a plain note card. I chose one that's cover said, "The words we most want to say are difficult to find sometimes. Their journey begins far, far, away in the heart." On the blank inside page I'd write some comforting words of my own. They might be hard to find, but they'd come from my heart.

Making Excuses

Often, the reason we excuse ourselves from contacting a hurting friend or acquaintance is because "I don't know what to say."

An acquaintance's husband dies, but we don't visit her or attend the funeral.

A friend's baby is born handicapped, but we keep silent.

A woman we know experiences a traumatic divorce, but we ignore her.

A couple we know files for bankruptcy, but we don't invite them over "in order to save them embarrassment."

"I wanted to call Diane, but I didn't know what to say."

"I knew I should have done something for them, but I didn't know what to do."

"I feel guilty because I didn't go over, but I didn't know what to say."

Do these comments sound familiar? Have they come from you? You wish you knew how to help your friends when they are experiencing difficult times, but you just don't.

Believing Fantasies

One reason we don't reach out to our friends may be that we've been programmed since childhood to believe the fairy tale that we'll all live happily ever after. Marriages are supposed to be "till death do us part." Money is supposed to increase every year. Babies are supposed to be born pretty and perfect. The Angel of Death is supposed to pass over the homes of the righteous.

So we hope for the best and avert our eyes from the possible tragedies of life. We're simply not equipped to face these experiences. Is it any wonder that when the unexpected occurs, we don't know what to say?

I ached inside when I received a phone call from my dad telling me that our friend Arne Obel had been killed in a small plane crash. *This can't be.* Arne was a warm, loving husband. His wife, Nina Jean, was devoted to him. *Why this tragedy? Why now?* It didn't seem fair. *Why must we be tested like this?*

Needing to Learn

"This is exactly what we need," my friend Terri said

when I told her that I was writing a book on comforting the hurting. "Yesterday, I talked with my mom. She said, 'My neighbor's son is in a coma in the hospital and I know I should call her, but I guess I'm just a coward. I don't know what to say.' "

We do want to comfort our friends, to help meet their needs, but we feel totally unprepared to do so. Each of us *can* become a more effective comforter, however. We *can* know what to say.

2

Tears That Taught Me How to Comfort

"What would a young girl like you know about suffering?" former Secretary of the Interior James Watt asked me at the Christian Bookseller's Convention. He listened as I told him my experiences. After a short time, he said, "That's enough. I believe you know what it is to hurt."

For me, hurting began early and centered around the thing I wanted most—to be a mother. I treated my dolls as though they were my babies. "Pitiful Pearl" was my favorite because she looked like she needed to be loved.

When I was four, a new baby arrived. I was thrilled to have Marita instead of a doll. Every morning I got up and helped my mother. I heated Marita's bottle, fed, her, changed her diapers, and then watched over her to make sure she didn't get into any trouble.

About a year and a half after Marita's arrival, my

parents brought home another new baby. Frederick Jerome Littauer III, my father's namesake, had his beautiful blue eyes, pale blonde hair and gorgeous dimples.

I cared for Freddie just as I had Marita, feeding, rocking, and dressing him. But when he was six-months-old, we realized that he wasn't progressing the way a normal child should. He began screaming in the middle of the night. Mother and I would meet in the hallway running to help him. All I could think was, *My baby is hurting!*

Mom and I held his stiffened body, pacing the floor, until he eventually relaxed and returned to sleep.

These nightly sessions finally sent us to the doctor's office. I held Freddie in the waiting room until it was our turn to enter, then stood anxiously in the background while Dr. Granger, the pediatrician, examined him.

After conferring with a neurologist, Dr. Granger told Mother, "I don't know how to tell you this, but your son is hopelessly brain-damaged. You might as well put him away, forget about him and maybe have another child."

Our baby hopeless? I couldn't believe it! I kept asking myself, *Why did this have to happen? Why wasn't my baby brother going to be like all the other children I'd seen?* Mom and Dad had always taught me to work hard and that I could do almost anything I wanted. But here was something no amount of work could change. Unknown to my parents, following that discovery, I hid in my room and cried.

Doctors reassured my parents that this would never happen again, so they decided to have another child. A year and a half later, Laurence was born. In the meantime, caring for Freddie, who was having 10 to

12 convulsions a day, was becoming increasingly difficult.

It was while mother was in the hospital delivering Larry that Dad put his namesake, Frederick III, into a private children's hospital where he could receive round-the-clock care. I had no idea what had happened to Freddie. He had just disappeared! *Where was he? Was he being taken care of? Was he loved?*

I never saw Freddie again. Five months after he was institutionalized, he died of pneumonia. Because of his severe brain-damage, he couldn't cough and choked to death in the night.

Both mother and I put all our efforts into nurturing Larry to ensure nothing could go wrong with him. We never discussed our enormous feelings of hurt and deprivation over losing Freddie. We just prayed that Larry would be everything Freddie couldn't be.

Tragedy Again

One week after Freddie died, Mom went into Larry's room to wake him from his nap. But he just lay there, expressionless and limp. Terrified that the nightmare was repeating itself, I insisted on accompanying her to the doctor's office.

After he examined Larry, Dr. Granger turned to mother. "I can't believe it. He's got the same thing. He's hopelessly brain-damaged."

I felt sick inside. *Isn't there something we can do?* I kept thinking over and over. Mom spoke up, "We've caught this one earlier. Maybe there's some hope."

But there was no hope. Larry grew steadily worse. Surgery at Johns Hopkins Metabolic Research Unit in Baltimore, Maryland, when he was one-year-old revealed that his brain was a nonfunctioning mass.

No hope! I cried when I saw Larry's bandaged head, swollen beyond recognition. *How could this have happened a second time?*

Blind and deaf, Larry never grew or changed after his surgery. His crying and convulsions continued.

One afternoon as I was playing at my friend's house, I glanced out the window to see Mom and Dad backing out of the driveway. I ran outside in time to find out that they were taking Larry away to the same children's hospital where Freddie had died just one year before. I never saw him again.

Silent Suffering

I could see that these traumas were destroying my parents, so I kept most of my feelings to myself. When kids at school called my brothers "morons," I never told Mom and Dad. No one knew how personally I'd taken these losses or how much I missed my two brothers.

My parents never mentioned the babies again, and we tried desperately to pretend we'd never had them. Since Larry was nothing but a living vegetable, Father decided it was best that we not see him again and remember him as he'd been. Privately, though, I would think of them often. I'd remember their birthdates. *How old would Freddie be? How old would Larry be?*

Sometimes in the evenings when I practiced the piano, I'd play a song from *The Music Man* "Goodnight My Someone," and sing it to Larry somewhere in a hospital that I'd never seen.

> Goodnight, my someone, Goodnight, my love.
> Sleep tight my someone, sleep tight my love.

Our star is shining its brightest light,
   for goodnight, my love, for goodnight.
Sweet dreams be yours dear, if dreams there
   be;
Sweet dreams to carry you close to me.
I wish they may and I wish they might.
Now goodnight, my someone, goodnight.
True love can be whispered from heart to
   heart,
When lovers are parted they say,
But I must depend on a wish and a star
As long as my heart, doesn't know where
   you are.
Goodnight my someone...

Grieving for Larry

Despite doctors' predictions that Larry would die
before his fifth birthday, he lived to be 19-years-old.
When he died, he was still the same size he'd been
when he was a year old. He never developed at all.

Even though I was a mother myself by then, his death
was far more difficult for me than I anticipated. He
hadn't been an integral part of our home, but he was
my brother. I had to grieve for him. His death was
especially hard for me because I had been trying to
discover the cause of my brothers' illness. When Larry
died, I gave up hope of finding out if his condition was
hereditary or not.

Marriage and Loss

In 1975, I married Randy Briggs. His mother had
suffered from multiple sclerosis for years. After we'd

been married a year, she became bedridden. I ached to watch such a beautiful, vivacious woman deteriorate. Despite extensive therapy and medical efforts, she died in 1977, before we had any children. At her death I grieved for my own loss, and also that she'd never have the chance to be the grandmother she'd always dreamed of being, and that she'd never be part of our children's lives.

New Life

On February 27, 1978, one year after her death, I gave birth to James Randall Briggs, Jr. New life in the Briggs family! Loving and caring for my very own baby was the happiest time in my life.

At six-months, the time when my brothers' problems had been discovered, Randy awoke screaming in the middle of the night. As I held him I prayed, "Lord, You can't let this happen again!" But gratefully, after three nights, he slept peacefully again.

Another Loss

Randy was about two-years-old when my husband and I decided we'd love to have another child. I became pregnant, but at five months, I lost the baby. Examination of the fetus revealed that my baby girl had severe abnormalities. I was shaken to the core. *My baby? There was something wrong with my baby?* Even though it wasn't what my brothers had, *could it possibly be related? Why did this happen? Why was I denied this child to raise?*

My time in the hospital compounded my grief. Every two hours when a nurse came in, turned on the fetal monitor and listened to my roommate's baby's heartbeat, I cringed in pain. That mother-to-be complained constantly about her discomfort and said she regretted getting pregnant. *Why did I have to lose the baby I cherished when she didn't care about hers?*

Continual hospital mixups intensified my misery. A nurse came in and asked, "Did you have a boy or girl?" *Hadn't she read my chart? Didn't she know my baby had died?*

A nutritionist asked, "Will you be nursing your baby?" An aide popped in and said gaily, "Your baby will be coming to be nursed soon." *How could such heartbreaking errors be made? Didn't anyone know why I was there? Didn't anyone care?*

The day I went home, the realization hit me that I was leaving empty-handed, without a baby in my arms. Devastated, I tried hard to be strong and not show how upset and angry I was.

Even focusing my thoughts on Randy, Jr. and the joy he gave us, couldn't compensate for the child I'd lost. Everything seemed to remind me—from my overweight condition to the boxes of baby clothes I had to pack away.

Moreover, some of the things people said only made me feel worse, like "Just be thankful you have Randy, Jr." "At least you can always try again," and "Don't you think it was all for the best?" No one, not even my family, understood how deeply I was hurting.

Finding Help

Months later, when my overwhelming feeling of loss diminished, I began to wonder, *Did other women have these feelings?* My physicians and genetic counselor said my reactions were very similar to others in my situation. I contacted a few other women who'd lost their babies mid-term and as we visited, we realized no one understood what a major loss we'd felt unless they'd been through it. Nothing was being done for women in our position. Later, I was instrumental in forming a support group for parents who've lost their babies mid-term. In the appendix I've included tips on how to form such a group for those who are grieving.

Blessing

One year after my miscarriage, I gave birth to our second son, Jonathan Laurence Briggs, who is a beautiful, healthy child.

And Sorrow

While writing this book, I suffered another loss, my 85-year-old grandmother passed away after a long bout with cancer. She lived in our home almost three years before she died.

Although she had a full life and is with the Lord, we still miss her. Often I expect to see her sitting in her chair by the window hulling the strawberries we grow in our yard or crocheting an afghan. She was a gentle woman who always had time for me and my children.

It's because of the losses I've experienced that I've become sensitive to the feelings of friends who endure traumatic times in their own lives. From these experiences as well as those of others with whom I've talked, I've learned things to do to help a grieving person and things to avoid. In succeeding chapters, I'll share what I've learned with you.

One thing I know: those who hurt desperately need comforters. Whether or not you have suffered the way your hurting friends have, you can be the person who helps them through. Serving as a comforter isn't easy, but it is one of the ministries needed most in the twentieth century.

3

Understanding the Hurting

My Grief

No!
  Disbelief.
Why?
  Shock.
Why?
  Anger.
Why?
  Guilt.
Why?
  Cheated.
Why?
  Loneliness,
  such loneliness.
Why?

Gladys Chmiel

When a man in our church died suddenly from a heart attack his family was crushed. Mr. Gregory had retired just that year; he and his wife had been busily planning things they wanted to do together. Now Mrs. Gregory felt as though life had come crashing down around her. Nothing would ever be the same.

Each day her life was affected in a different way by her loss. Her husband had always taken care of their financial matters. She'd never worked outside the home. And, although she enjoyed gardening, she wasn't able to do the heavy yard work. As each day passed, she seemed to miss him in a new way.

A major void had been created in Mrs. Gregory's life. *What is there left to live for?* she thought.

What the Words Mean

To effectively comfort someone like Mrs. Gregory, we need to understand what the hurting person is experiencing and feeling. One of the ways to do that is to understand the descriptive terms associated with their plight.

1. *Loss.* Anything that falls short of realistic expectations is loss. It is also "being deprived of or being without something one has had and has valued."[1] Both definitions show that people can experience loss at many different levels—from losing a tooth to losing a loved one.

2. *Grief.* Grief is a deep sadness, intense emotional suffering, acute sorrow caused by *loss.*

3. *Mourning.* This word encompasses the external signs of *grief,* such as the funeral, the wearing of black, and a withdrawal from public. Mourning varies according to cultural background, personal beliefs, and societal pressures.

Types of Loss and Response

There are two types of loss: predictable and unexpected. Whenever there has been a loss of any kind a person will experience the normal stages of grief. Whether that sense of loss is only momentary, as in a missed phone call or years, as with a death or divorce—any loss results in grief. It's the severity that differs. With a predictable loss like the anticipated death of a terminally ill person, some of the grieving begins before the person dies. If the person is elderly, because of their age, it may be expected and may even seem benign.

When the death is unexpected—like one that is the result of an accident or that of a stillborn child, it may seem especially unfair. And if any loss is connected with past experiences, the current event will seem even more extreme.

Some situations are not as firmly resolved as death is. In a divorce, for example the relationship has changed but the mate or parent is alive. The husband is no longer part of the wife's life, but because of the children she may still see him occasionally.

And once a person suffers a loss, they know that they are vulnerable. *It happened once; it could happen again.* Your husband doesn't come home from work on time, and you think, *He's in an accident.* You remember how it was when your father died. *Maybe it's happened again.*

Everyone who loves is vulnerable to the pain of grief. Love means attachment and all human attachments are subject to loss. Our responsibility as comforters is to be sensitive to various forms of loss and to the ways each individual is reacting to his own loss.

What are some of the different experiences our friends, loved ones—even we ourselves—are apt to face?

Loss of a Significant Person

A significant person may be one's spouse, as it was for Mrs. Gregory. Or it may be a close friend, parent, child, relative, or anyone who has made a major impact on one's life. They've been part of us, we've valued them, and now they're gone.

Loss of Pregnancy or Newborn

A miscarriage, premature birth, stillbirth, or death of an infant is the loss of a significant person. But it's important to differentiate between this and the death of an adult. While both are major losses, a child's death is the end of parental dreams that will never be fulfilled.

When her baby was stillborn, Lisa's life became empty and meaningless. She felt that no one understood how attached she'd become to the new life inside her. For months, she'd decorated the nursery, bought the layette, and talked to her baby about the life they'd have together.

One close friend's comment, "Oh, Lisa, you're so young. I'm sure you'll be pregnant again real soon," only indicated that she didn't understand Lisa's loss or her emotional distress. Whether or not she'd have another baby wasn't important to her now. What mattered was that her baby was dead and she'd been denied the future she'd dreamed of.

Often no one shares the feelings of this kind of loss except the immediate family. Individuals outside the family do not realize what a severe blow this is; it is an event that has caused the couple to fall short of their realistic expectations.

Loss of a Physical Part of Self

Loss of a body part can happen in two ways. One is a structural loss such as an amputation or a mastectomy. The other is a loss of a body function such as blindness or paralysis. In both of these cases, the individual is deprived of something they've had and valued. Both will result in a grief reaction.

Mike is a jewelry engraver. He fell through a glass display case, cutting all the nerves in his right arm. The recovery process has been very slow. He may never regain full use of his hand and, as a result, may be unable to engrave again.

When George fell off the ladder, severed his spinal cord, and knew he'd never walk again, he thought his life was over. No longer could he do most of the things he'd done so easily before. It took years of therapy for him to relearn a few minimal tasks. Both Mike and George had to work through all their feelings of loss and grieve for the life they once had.

Sherry had a radical mastectomy when she was 29, before she had children. Not only was she shattered by the visual loss of her breasts but also at the thought that she'd never be able to nurse a baby. "I'm so young," she mourned. "It is so unfair."

Birth of a Developmentally Disabled Child

When a couple gives birth to a child with a physical or mental handicap, they experience the loss of the anticipated healthy child.

When Jennifer was told that Damian had cerebral palsy, she had to give up her dreams of the things her baby would do. During her pregnancy she'd see a child climbing a tree and look forward to the time her baby would do that. She'd wonder, *If it's a girl, will she take ballet? If it's a boy, will he play football? Will my child win the class spelling bee?*

As the reality of Damian's disability set in, she was forced to rethink all her expectations and dreams. She tried to hope for the best and provide the warmth she knew her child would need. But her husband, Jack, rejected their son. Every evening when he came home from work, he ignored the boy, never holding him or even asking how he'd been that day.

Despite Jennifer's efforts, the marriage ended in divorce because Jack could never face Damian's disability. Their son had fallen short of their realistic expectations.

Loss of a Loved One Due to Lingering Illness

Death of a loved one due to a lingering illness will carry with it all the characteristics of the loss of a significant person. But it will vary because the family will be experiencing anticipatory grief, the term applied to grief expressed in advance of a loss when the death is perceived inevitable.[2] This family will need uplifting and support all during the illness as well as following the death.

Betty Lou had been caring for her terminally ill husband and her aging mother for years. When they both died within six months of each other, people commented, "What a relief this must be for you."

It was a relief of physical work and responsibility, but they were major losses too. She was very lonely following their deaths. Even when death is seen as a relief, the survivors have lost their loved one. Often their purpose for living and their feeling of being needed has been eliminated.

Loss of a Spouse by Divorce

The loss of a spouse through divorce is just as difficult as it is in death and may even be more devastating. Death is final and irreversible. In a divorce their lives go on, but no longer in the same relationship. It is this change in relationship that is traumatic. In addition, while in death one loses the person loved, in divorce, one's love has been rejected.

It is painful for Jo Ann to know that not only has her husband rejected her love, but that now he's giving it to his new girlfriend. Every time Bill comes by to pick up the children, his girlfriend comes along, clinging to him as if to show how wonderful their new relationship is. After a year and a half, the pain has not let up. She can't stand to see her ex-husband giving to someone else what he used to give to her.

The deserted partner is apt to feel the same loss and grief they would over a death. People like these need continued love and support before, during, and especially after the divorce. Their relationship has fallen short of their realistic expectations.

Loss of Possessions

Loss of valued possessions from theft, fire, or financial problems often has long term, painful effects. Barbara's house was hit by a fireball during the California Panorama Fire. The fireball exploded into flames and burned their home to the ground.

People tried to cheer her up. "Just think, now you can start all over again. Won't that be fun?" But to Barbara, their words seemed callous as she recalled all the family memories that had been created in that house, the baby pictures that were destroyed, and the hours and love she'd poured into making it their home. Those were things insurance money could never replace.

Imagine how you'd feel if every possession you had was snatched away with no warning. As comforters, we're not to moralize as to whether these things *should* be valued. Instead, we're to realize that a loss has taken place and the individual needs our comfort and support.

Loss of a Friend by Relocation

When a friend moves away, you lose a valued relationship because of the distance between you. Janell told me that when her spiritual sister moved away, it was like having her arm cut off. "Our relationship was something special that I don't expect to replace. There will be other close friends but probably not the nurturing friendship Ruth Ann and I shared. Our closeness and intimacy have now been diminished." Ruth Ann was someone Janell could bare her soul to, a refuge where she'd receive unconditional love.

Loss of a Pet

When a much-loved pet runs away or dies, the resulting grief is no less real. Moni was our first dog whom we had before our children were born. One morning she began having convulsions and we rushed her to the veterinarian. She survived for three days, when her liver failed and she died. When Moni died, I cried for days. I kept hearing her bark and would expect to see her sleeping on the couch as I walked into the family room.

Months later, we purchased a new schnauzer who looked just like Moni; she even had some of the same champions in her pedigree. We look at her and expect her to be Moni, but she is not. She doesn't respond to us the way Moni did. She's a new and different dog.

An emotional response to the loss of a pet can be increased if there have been other significant losses in the family's lives already. When my own pets died, it brought back all the other hurts I'd had in my life. This just added one more to them.

Under normal circumstances an adult does not grieve over a pet very long. However, when there have been suppressed past losses, as I had from losing my brothers, the person may grieve beyond what might be expected. Be sensitive to your friends' sadness when they've lost a pet. Remember that this may bring up past losses in their lives. Ask them to share how they really feel. Listen. Don't tell them it's foolish to cry over a dog.

Each of the preceeding experiences—from death of a significant person to the death of a pet—is heartfelt to the individual to whom it happens. Your understanding of the nature and depth of their grief in each situation will enable you to become the empathetic comforter they need.

4

Becoming Comforters

Faith Broken

Oh, God, I am so confused.
I have loved you so much.
How difficult this has been to understand.
I have felt my faith broken, but I struggle to
    regain it.
For I know you are my God, and you have
    not forsaken me.
Lead me where I need to walk, and let my
    faith be built anew.

Gladys Chmiel

Nancy's baby had died three days after his premature birth, and she lay despondent on her hospital bed. It was the end of the day and her doctor, who was on his way home, walked into the room. He talked with her about her son's medical complications and resulting death. When he was about to leave he asked, "Do you have any other questions about what happened?"

Nancy thought a moment, then blurted out, "I do have one question. Why won't anyone talk to me?"

"Who won't talk to you," he asked, surprised. "Is it the other doctors? The hospital staff? Your family and friends?"

"No one really talks to me. When the nurse comes in, she takes my blood pressure and leaves. The doctors check me to see how I am physically. My family asks a polite, 'How are you?' and then tells me what everyone else is doing. My friends haven't come to see me, except for a few, and those that have come by don't talk with me. They just act happy and tell me what's going on in their world."

"I'll be honest with you, Nancy. We all hurt for you so much we just don't know what to say. When I've finished a long day caring for critically ill newborns and walk out of the nursery, I have a choice. I can turn left and go home to my family where there's happiness, fun and relaxation, or I can turn right, come down here to your room and share your pain. Quite frankly, it's easier to go home."

The Hurting Need Comforters

It is easier to go home and ignore the hurting ones. It's easier just to pray that God will be a comfort to your bereaved friend. It takes effort to express caring. It takes work to be supportive. It takes time to be a comforter. But that's what your suffering friend needs.

Why reach out and support one another? Because

God says so. "Comfort, comfort my people,"
in Isaiah 40:1 (NIV). "These are my people;
them for me," He exhorts.

In Isaiah 66:13 He puts it this way. "As a
comforts her child, so will I comfort you;" (NIV). But
how many have seen God Himself walk into the room?
He does comfort through His Holy Spirit within. But
He also needs human beings through whom He can
work.

So many of God's people need help. They have lost
loved ones, jobs, money, valued relationships, and
homes. They are ill or facing surgery. They are divorced, widowed, or lonely. God needs us to be His
arms around those who hurt. Although He is their inner
and ultimate strength, He calls on us to meet their
physical and emotional needs in time of crisis.

Profile of a Comforter

A comforter does not have to go to Comfort School.
He does need to be compassionate—to sympathize with
others' distresses and desire to alleviate them. If you're
a comforter be warm, empathetic, and have a sympathetic ear. Encourage those who hurt to ventilate and
deal with their feelings. Offer positive feedback about
what they are thinking and saying. Approach them with
enthusiasm, out of genuine love for the family and
sincere concern for each one.

Develop Your Special Abilities

One friend told me, "I'm sure glad you like to help
people when they are grieving, because it certainly isn't
my gift." I'm not sure it's my gift either, but I've
learned to drop everything and go in obedience to

God whether or not I feel like it or it's convenient.

I'm not suggesting everyone needs to weep with the hurting. If your strength is to be of a sound mind in a crisis, then you can be that strength for them in the middle of their crisis. If you are emotional, you can be the understanding person they need to cry with.

We each need to develop our God-given assets and demonstrate the qualities of a comforter so we can minister effectively.

So don't hesitate to get involved in meeting a family's needs—especially if you have suffered in a similar fashion. It isn't even necessary to be a close friend. Your understanding will be special.

How Not to Help

Don't try to answer their "why's." Job's three friends tried to do that. "I have heard many things like these:" he told them in disgust. "Miserable comforters are you all!" (Job 16:1,2 NIV).

None of us could have answered Job's "why's." God did use his experiences to teach succeeding generations many things. But is that why Job endured such traumatic losses?

The explanations his comforters were offering him included statements like, "There must be sin in your life." "You must not have enough faith." "God must be trying to teach you something." "I'm sure you will forget about your trouble." "You must be blessed because God has chosen to discipline you."

I cried out to God and asked why my brother had to have such serious brain damage. Why did the same thing have to happen again? Why did one brother die at an early age, while the second lingered as a vegetable for almost 20 years? Why did my family have to face financial difficulty? Why did my mother-in-law get multiple schlerosis and die so young? Why did my second pregnancy have a severe abnormality? Why did my grandmother get cancer?

If you had been trying to comfort me, would you tell me that it was God's will for me to go through so many tragedies by the time I was 29-years-old? I don't know why all these things happened, but I do know that God is in control of my life. God has used these experiences to work in my life and have an impact on the world around me. Lives have been touched as a result of my response to these traumas. So I trust God for His strength and guidance. But that does not answer my "why's."

We live in an imperfect world that has been affected by sin. God did not create heaven and earth in order that man would live there in heartache and grief. Man was given a choice whether or not to obey God. Man chose to disobey, and as a result, sin became part of our world. Does that mean God makes all the bad things happen? Theologians have been debating that issue for centuries.

Be Understanding

It's natural to ask "Why?" when life seems to deal you a crucial blow. But it's important for us to realize that it's not our role to offer explanations. Nor is a tragedy the time to judge or criticize. We can emphathize instead, letting the person know that we feel with them and see their tragedy as real and painful.

One mother told me, "I don't know why God allowed Joshua to die. I have come to the point where I accept it and have stopped questioning. But I may not know why until I'm with Him. God has given me peace, and

I can share with others facing a similar loss. I can comfort them with the comfort God has given to me. Before Joshua died, heaven seemed so far away. Now, it seems so close."

Another mother I counseled called me at 10:30 one night in tears. She said, "I feel so cheated. Why did this have to happen to me?" She'd lost her baby at birth and had just spent the evening with an unmarried woman who was pregnant. All evening, she'd talked about how miserable she felt and about how unhappy she was to be having a baby. "It's not fair!" she told me. I listened and agreed with her. I didn't have answers, and would only have hurt her by offering explanations.

Accept your hurting person. As they progress through the myriad of questions that deluge them, encourage them to be honest with God about their feelings. He's the only one who can give them peace.

5

Difficult Decisions

The Verdict

The Verdict is in
I am guilty
I made the decision—
I gave the answer I always thought you would
   give me, Lord.
The decision I always thought you would
   make.
But I have had to do it.
And I am consumed by guilt.
Did I do the right thing?
Did I make the right choice?
Can I live with what I've done?
I cry out in the night to know the answer!
Will I ever know?

I will never be the same.
The verdict is in.
I am guilty.

Gladys Chmiel

I'd just walked in the door after taking Randy, Jr. to school. My husband was hanging up the phone. "It's bad news. Grammy was found unresponsive in her bed this morning and is being rushed to the hospital." Leaving our two-year-old son, Jonathan, with a neighbor, we hurried to her.

My 85-year-old grandmother had lived with us for three years, and had been battling melanoma, a kind of cancer, for five. Just two months before, she'd moved to a retirement home two miles away where she could be looked after 24-hours-a-day.

Is this the final hour? we wondered. *Or was it a minor problem that would be resolved with medical treatment?*

Grammy was being taken out of the ambulance when we arrived at the emergency room. She was whisked off to an examining room while I filled out the necessary forms. Then we were told to wait in an adjoining room.

Moments later, we were called in by her doctor. His first statement left me feeling helpless. "I need you to tell me how aggressive you want us to be."

Of course I wanted her to be treated and cared for! But how could I determine how "aggressive" they should be? The doctor became more specific. "If she stops breathing, should we put her on a respirator? If she experiences cardiac arrest, should we try to stimulate her?"

Grammy didn't want to be "kept alive" by machine, I knew that. But I had to make a decision—one we'd always thought God would make. That moment, Randy and I had to respond the way we felt Grammy and her children would want us to.

I had peace that if Grammy were standing between us, that she'd say, "Let me go! I'm tired of fighting. I'm ready. Please let me go."

Randy and I knew we were speaking for Grammy and her children when we said, "No respirator, no heart machine, and no extraordinary measures to keep her alive."

"I'm sure it's for the best," her doctor told us. "Her struggle with melanoma would only be a downhill road. It isn't controlled. She has had a stroke and is in a coma. I feel she has only hours to days, not weeks to months, to live."

I felt strange discussing Grammy's life and death so casually and intellectually, and yet, we knew it was what she wanted. Now that we'd decided not to sustain her life with support systems, the waiting began. Although her condition had stabilized, she was not responding or improving. Throughout the day, she continued breathing on her own, but did not regain consciousness.

That evening, her physician told us that Grammy probably wouldn't live through the night. But by morning, she was still alive. Her breathing had become more labored, however, and we knew this was truly her final hour. By noon her son arrived from Dallas, Texas and made the final decision that no life sustaining measures be taken. At 3:00 P.M., with her son at her side, she passed away peacefully.

Scientific advances in today's world have forced us to make decisions people have never had to make before. If your hurting person has had to do that, you'll need to be aware of the emotions he's experiencing. Even making the "right" decision, doesn't make it easy to do. Those individuals need your loving support without a hint of judgment.

Tough Choices

What kind of decisions are people facing today? They can be divided into two categories: those which affect the physical life of a loved one and those which affect their emotions. The ones that affect physical life include things like halting efforts to keep a premature baby alive, ending chemotherapy treatments, or pulling the plug on life-support systems.

It is not my position to tell someone else what to do at a time like this. It is important to not offer opinions or make judgments.

Consider the feelings of a family whose premature baby is barely being kept alive. He has severe brain damage, a weakened heart, and poor lung development. While the baby might survive necessary heart surgery, due to the other factors, he would never be normal and would probably spend his life institutionalized.

Imagine how family members attempting to make this kind of decision feel. Do they insist everything possible be done to keep the baby alive? Or do they request that no extraordinary measures be taken and allow the baby to live or die according to its own ability?

A woman who is four months pregnant goes in for a routine sonogram of her baby and learns that the child has no brain and that it cannot survive outside the womb. She is asked to decide whether doctors should induce premature labor or if she should carry her baby for another five months, knowing he will die at birth.

A 45-year-old woman with two teenaged children has been told that she has breast cancer and that it has already spread through the lymph system. She is given six months to live. Chemotheraphy might extend her life another six months.

The woman and her family must now decide whether she should take the chemotheraphy (with all its side effects) to add some time to her life. Or should she allow things to take their natural course and intervene as little as possible?

A teenaged son lies comatose in the emergency room following a severe car accident. Indications are that he will not survive. However, exploratory surgery could be performed to find the true extent of the injuries.

"You're son's condition is touch and go," the family is told. "He'll never be the same." They must decide to consent or not.

A 60-year-old husband and father has suffered a major heart attack and is on a respirator. The doctor informs the family that there has been extensive damage. Most likely he won't regain consciousness or be able to live without the respirator. How long do they want him to be "kept alive"?

Pray for Them

There are many other situations like these that require a decision. Some may seem clear, but often they are painful and difficult. Rarely are they ever easy.

As comforters, we must uphold our friends in prayer before they make the decision, while it is being carried out, and afterwards as well. In addition, let's provide them with nonjudgmental and unconditional support.

Other Ways to Help with Guilt

One of the natural reactions to making such painful choices is guilt. That guilt may be genuine—the result of something for which the individual is responsible, or it may be unjustified. In any event, it is a natural response to making these kinds of decisions. The persons ask themselves, *Did I make the right choice?*

Whether your hurting person is experiencing justifiable or false guilt, we need to be aware that those feelings are very real and should be discussed. As the grief process takes place, encourage him to share his thoughts.

Never respond by saying, "Oh, you shouldn't feel that way." The truth is that they *do* feel that way and need your understanding and compassion. If they are experiencing justifiable guilt, encourage them by talking about God's forgiveness and unconditional love.

Even decisions which don't affect physical life are hard to make and can be traumatic. Consider the wife and mother, who, after two years of earnest marriage counseling, is served with divorce papers. She is asked to sign that she agrees with their statements. Is she to continue to live in emotional turmoil, refusing to agree to her husband's demands? Is she to face months of court battles over money and custody? Or is she to agree to something she doesn't want?

Dealing with Hindsight

Guilt can be the result of a person's "if only's". "If only I hadn't said those things to him." "If only I had called the doctor sooner." "If only I wasn't working then, this would never have happened."

It's easy to feel guilty about some of the things we did or did not do when a loved one dies. The finality of death destroys the possibility of righting any wrongs toward the person.

How do we help such individuals? There may be nothing we can say to resolve the problem. We can pray that God will give them the insight they need. And we can stay with them, communicating His love, for as long as they need us.

6

The First Two Steps in Comforting

There are three things a comforter needs to do for someone who is experiencing a loss. First, acknowledge that such a thing has taken place. That is simpler to do when there has been a death than in other situations where the loss is harder to identify.

One woman told me she'd miscarried about mid-term in her pregnancy. Five weeks after that event, not one person had even acknowledged her loss. Her friends avoided the issue, trying to sweep it aside either as insignificant or because they didn't want her to focus on it.

Second, we need to allow the hurting to express their grief normally and appropriately. As their grief is dealt with, they will begin to come to a healthy resolution, the final step of any experience of loss. As comforters, we can help them do that.

As we accompany our friends through these steps, the most important thing we can do is to *be understanding*. Are we aware of what they're going through? Are we trying to find easy solutions to their pain? Are we telling them to forget the past—to get done with their grief, and then quoting a few Scriptures to them? What we need instead is to realize how deeply they hurt and how to help.

Acknowledging Their Loss

The first step the bereaved must take is to acknowledge their loss, not pretend it hasn't happened. When the tragedy is the loss of a loved one, call the bereaved person and say, "I just heard of your brother's death. I'm so sorry this has happened. I want you to know that I love you and share your loss with you. I'm praying for you. Is there something specific you'd like me to pray about for you or your family?"

Never just say, "I'm sorry," and wait for him to respond. What can he say in return, "I'm sorry, too," or "Thank you"? Ask leading questions that will give him the opportunity to let you know his needs and feelings.

Often in the middle of a crisis, there'll be someone at the house shielding the bereaved person from phone calls. If it isn't appropriate for you to talk to the one who's experienced a loss, leave a message that you've called and are praying for him. Be sure to state your relationship to the family.

Another way to acknowledge his loss is to visit him. Personal contact allows him to see that you share his pain. If you choose this method of acknowledging his loss, give him a hug and offer your support.

Making the First Contact

Close friends should phone the bereaved person immediately and stop by as soon as possible. Acquaintances or co-workers who are not intimate friends should do whatever is appropriate: Go to the funeral home, attend the funeral, or send a sympathy card.

Helping the Hurting Person Express His Grief

Grieving is the second phase of the loss experience, and comforters need to help the bereaved do that normally and appropriately. This is a long, broad phase involving all aspects of grief and may include shock, denial, anger, bitterness, guilt, loneliness, depression, adjustment, and acceptance.

It's not up to us to decide what's the right way for others to grieve. They may be appropriately sad and immersed in their grief. Allow them to focus inwardly and try to understand what they are feeling. They may cry. Let them do that. They may question God and ask, "Why did this happen to me?" These are normal reactions, and they'll vary. We'll help immeasurably if we give them the time they need and stay close to them during the process.

It's important to remember that your friend *must* acknowledge that a loss has taken place before he grieves. He may not be able to face any other phase of grieving for a week, a month or even longer. Don't rush him. There's no set amount of time anyone stays on one step.

The following are brief descriptions of the various stages of grief that your friend may face.

Shock and Denial

Their first reaction to a loss will probably be to cry, "No! This can't be!" That's what I think when someone I know has been in an accident. *Maybe he really wasn't in that car. Maybe it was someone else,* I hope unrealistically. A defense or coping mechanism takes over the shocked person when they first hear some unbearable news. It may create a numbness, be a buffer, or cause a lack of awareness of the situation.

This natural reaction acts as an anesthetic and should not be viewed negatively. Protective, it allows the person to face the tragedy gradually, as God provides strength. Otherwise, the fact that his world has come to a screeching halt and will never be the same again would be unbearable.

Anger and Questioning

Your friend may face periods of anger and questioning. He or she may be angry at God for allowing such a senseless event to occur, angry at the world in general, angry at themselves for some flaw in their character which they feel may have been the cause of the tragedy. They may be very sensitive and react in anger to those who say foolish and thoughtless things or they may ignore them.

I remember how upset I became with the nurse who asked me if I had a boy or a girl after I'd just lost my baby. They'll often search for reasons why this happened to them. They can't understand why a loving God would allow such a tragedy to happen.

Guilt

No matter how the loss occurred, there'll be some feelings of guilt. While occasionally it may be genuine, most is unjustified. False guilt is one of the normal responses of grief.

If you're with someone who feels that way, remember that it's very real to him and should not be dismissed. Discuss his feelings with him without judging or belittling. The person is asking himself, *Was I responsible in some way? Could I have done something to prevent it? Is God trying to punish me for some past sin in my life?* Common questions after a loss, they are usually accompanied by bitterness and sadness.

Depression and Loneliness

Even if the bereaved is surrounded by caring and supportive family and friends, he may still have feelings of loneliness and depression. A time may come when your friend sees no reason to go on living. *I'm all alone. No one understands how much I hurt.* These feelings are almost unavoidable, and may surface regardless of their spirituality.

These feelings of depression and loneliness and the hurting person's call for help is beautifully described by Christine Wyrtzen in her song, "Carry Me."

> My family has come with words to console,
> And friends have been calling on the telephone.
> In spite of the well-meaning words they've all given,
> I can't help but feel that I'm standing alone.

Lord, I do have some feelings I want to
   confide,
I feel so alone though my friends offer
   smiles.
It's only your love that can carry the hurt.
May I ask you to hold me for a few painful
   miles?

Carry me, won't you carry me now?
I'm too weak and fragile to walk on my own.
I'll rest in your love till once more I can stand.
To journey beside you and follow you home.

7

The Third Step

Everyone has tunnel vision when he is grieving, but there will come a time when he sees a tiny light at the end of that tunnel. With a glimmer of hope, he realizes that the pain is diminishing and there is a new beginning on the horizon. Your role during this state is to guide him through his grief and enable him to see that there is a reason to go on. "There is life beyond the hurt you're experiencing now. You can live without your loved one."

It's hard for a comforter to sit and endure all their friend's sorrow. Often, they just want to pick up that person and move them over to an acceptance of their loss. They may indicate this by comments such as, "But we know all things work together for good."

The things which your suffering friend is going

through may work together for some good someday, but right now it's very difficult for him to see any good in his loss. He hurts. He's sad. He cries. What he needs is for you to share his sorrow with him. Whatever it takes, however long it takes, be there with him. Allow him to work through all the stages of grief. It must take place. It cannot be hurried. As this grieving does take place, gradually—very gradually—the hurting person will move toward resolution.

A Healthy Resolution

Bit by bit, as the bereaved come to this third and final phase, the pain will begin to diminish and he'll start to see life outside his own sadness again. For some people it may take a week or two before they begin to see a healthy resolution. For others it could be six months or a year before they find themselves heading towards an acceptance of their loss.

Not Forgotten

After I lost my baby, Nancy told me, "Lauren, there will be some good days and some bad days."

Good days? I thought to myself, *I'd be thankful for a good hour when I'm not dwelling on my loss.*

But as the months went by, a day did come when my loss wasn't the first thing I thought about in the morning and the last thing I thought about before sleep at night. More months went by and I realized, "I haven't grieved over that now for about a week." I realized that what Nancy said was true. Things *were* getting better.

But as comforters, we must be aware that the

heartache is still there. Even though someone appears to have reached a resolution, still he'll have moments when he wells up with sadness. Some word brings back a vivid memory. Some circumstance makes him relive his own painful experience.

A parent who has lost a child may seem to have her life well under control and feel she's reached a healthy resolution. Then all of a sudden, a TV commercial airs in which a child is playing happily in a field with the wind blowing in her hair. The parent bursts into tears. How can she be so upset when she seemed to have worked through her loss?

The parent had worked through it, but she has been denied the raising of a child the way she had planned. So, although her focus has changed and the pain has diminished, the loss will never be completely forgotten.

There will be unexpected moments for the parents when they're not prepared to be reminded of their loss—moments when their emotions surface and they weep. One day when I was eight-months pregnant with my second son, Jonathan, and should have been joyous, I saw a baby girl that reminded me of the one I was denied. I burst into tears.

Why was I crying? Because, even though I was about to have another baby, I was feeling the loss of something I no longer had. The impending birth was exciting, but it couldn't replace the baby I had lost.

Know Where They're At

We are not therapists offering to counsel the hurting. Our role is to be understanding, loving, supportive friends. If you're sensitive enough to discern they're level of grief, that knowledge will help you comfort them and reassure the hurting that what they are experiencing is normal. Be careful not to say to the person, "I can tell you are in the guilty stage and I'm sure you'll get depressed soon."

When Nina Jean seemed to be handling her grief well, a friend said, "If you don't cry now, you'll have a nervous breakdown in six months." If the Lord gives someone a supernatural acceptance of her loss, be grateful.

Grieving Takes Work

Because grief is active, not passive, it takes both mental and emotional work. Not only must the hurting do that work—those who comfort must experience the work of grieving as well.

Grieving takes time. It takes time to heal the wound. The pain does lessen, but a permanent imprint is left in the memory and the hurt is changed by the experience. That which is lost is never forgotten. The acute grief will subside, but there may never be a substitute for the loss. The memory is a way of perpetuating the love that the hurt does not, and perhaps should not, want to relinquish.

After my father-in-law read the first few chapters of this book, he talked with me about his wife's life and death. "No matter how long the illness lasts, you are never prepared for death when it comes. Even now, seven years after she died, I find myself saying, 'Mary would have loved to have seen this' or 'That was always one of Mary's favorite songs.' I know that chapter in my life has ended, but I don't want to forget the 30 years we had together and all the beautiful memories of those times."

The following letter in which a mother who lost her baby mid-term shares some of her feelings and needs, exemplifies many of the aspects of loss I have just described.

Dear Friends,

I am most grateful for your package of articles and notes that you sent me. The majority of my therapy right now is reading about my problem and the grief that has so many aspects. The other part of my therapy is receiving phone calls and messages of condolence from friends who realize what a pitiful loss it was and are compassionate enough to let me talk about my feelings. I dread the day when the phone calls and the "How are you's" will stop, and I will be alone in my sorrow.

Tomorrow I will be forced to face a "friend" of mine who is pregnant and due two weeks ahead of when I would have been. The relationship with her will always be strained, for I am not strong enough to watch her experience what I was cheated of, and her child will always remind me of how old mine would have been. I believe my own emptiness will always set me apart from her, my mourning will always, necessarily, conflict with her joy.

Unfortunately this girl's son and my son are in the same pre-school, and tomorrow there will be a field trip. This girl did send me a condolence card, but somehow, her message that she hoped I would "soon be my cheery self" simply emphasized her simplicity and our differences.

...I was relieved to know that it is normal that my husband did not feel the same bonding that I had with my baby and that my preoccupation with my loss is an expected or common reaction, especially since my father has recently suggested that I put the experience on a "back burner" (when my loss was less than three weeks old!). I have learned that some people do not appreciate my grieving for very long. One other reaction that you did not address is...a fear of taking future risks and chances.

I especially appreciate your sending me a copy of one of the family's experiences. It was comforting to read someone else's account of what was almost my exact experience, to see my same opinions and emotions put into words, and to know someone else "has been there." It is so true that your entire world crashes around you and that the experience has a profound ongoing, permanent impact on your life. I also felt numb, helpless, bewildered, and depressed. When I think of the baby I lost, I picture my hopes and illusions about him. But in addition I will never be the same because a part of me died when he died.

I was thankful we had a funeral for him so that there is a tangible place to visit and be with my thoughts and feelings about him. I don't ever want to forget him. He was my third child and I want to always remember that he did exist. I miss him even though I never saw him.

I know this is all familiar to you, but I appreciate your giving me an opportunity to share my sadness with you. Thank you for understanding my needs and the depth of my pain.

Sincerely,

Sharon Rudi

8

Practical Ways to Help

My Friends

In the midst of the pain, your sun shone
    through.
Your words of comfort, your feelings of
    love, your issues of support.
How much they have meant.
You are so dear to me.
My love for you grows ever deeper.
I give you my thanks.

Gladys Chmiel

We have already established that hurting persons
need us. They need our time, prayers and love. The
next two chapters offer practical helps for those

who are bereaved following the death of their loved one, or in other crisis situations.

The family has so many things to tend to immediately after a death, that this is a perfect time for friends to mobilize and put their love and concern into action. You'll have to take the initiative, because often they're too confused to judge what needs to be done. One person can't do everything, so it's a good idea for one friend to coordinate the project and see that all needs are being filled.

How the Church Can Help

Our church has a family services ministry that springs into action whenever someone in our fellowship is hospitalized, a baby is born, or a traumatic situation occurs. One woman serves as the coordinator and finds out how many meals will be needed, whether there are any dietary specifications and what other things can be done for the family. The coordinator then calls volunteers to help with meals, babysitting, transportation and other services, and assigns the various needs to them. Providing services to a family during a time of crisis is an ideal way for a church to minister.

Provide Food

Remember that the family will need meals before, as well as after, the funeral service. Find out approximately how many people will be with the family during the days following the funeral, so there will be enough food. Ask volunteers what they're bringing or make suggestions to reduce duplication. Make sure that there is enough, as well as a variety, of food. Suggest that each person bringing a dish label it to make it easier to return.

Don't worry that there will be too much food. One widow said, "I had so much food I had to freeze some of it. But that has been such a blessing, because if someone is coming over I can just take a casserole out of the freezer and not worry about having to fix a meal."

Don't expect the bereaved to remember what you brought, even if you're a good friend. Your efforts won't go unnoticed, though. Following the death of her mother, Martha said, "Because people were preparing the meals, Dad ate. I know he wouldn't have eaten if he had been the one that had to cook."

If there's been a memorial service, a meal will probably follow. Make sure there's enough help to lay out the food, serve and clean up.

When my babysitter's elderly mother died, I didn't feel that I needed to go to the funeral, but I did want to help. I stayed at the house with the young grandchildren and got the buffet laid out so everything was ready when they got home. I stayed to serve the meal, kept fresh coffee supplied, the punch bowl filled, and food replenished.

Even though you may have arranged for meals to be prepared for the family, see that there are staples on hand such as milk, butter, coffee, eggs, bacon, and cream. Remember to plan for all the meals that will need to be served during the next few days, including breakfasts.

Carol told me of an embarrassing moment she had the day after her husband died. "My mother-in-law arrived that morning along with my brother and his wife. I went into the kitchen to fix a pot of coffee and found there was only a tablespoon left in the can. I realized that while my husband had been hospitalized over the past two weeks I had let all my supplies run down and I was low on most of my standard food items." Be sure to check regularly stocked items so that the family won't have to worry about it.

Provide Transportation

Family members may be flying in for the funeral and they'll need to be picked up at the airport. Although the bereaved may want to go themselves, they may be relieved to have you do it for them.

If the family needs an extra car for their visitors, find someone who can provide one. A member of our church sells used cars and lets people in the body borrow one during a crisis.

Find Lodging for Guests

If visiting relatives prefer to stay in the home and be with the family, check to see if that's what the family wants. If not, make other lodging arrangements. Out-of-towners may state ahead of time that they prefer to stay at a hotel. If so, you can make arrangements before they arrive.

Some may need a place to stay but may be unable to afford a hotel. Perhaps church families would be willing to have them as guests. Be sensitive to what the family wants, and try to facilitate that as much as possible.

Make Phone Calls

Many people will need to be called and informed. Ask family members whom they need to contact personally (they may need someone with them when they make these calls). Offer to call the rest of the people for them. But only make those calls with the family's permission.

Write down the basic information in order to be accurate. Say something like, "This is Lauren Briggs, the Johnson family has asked me to call to let you know that their son, Robert, was killed this morning in a car accident. Funeral services will be held at the Greenspot Mortuary, Tuesday at 2 P.M. and visitation will be there from 3 P.M. through 8 P.M. on Monday."

Offer to call the church prayer chain. If the family agrees, ask prayer chain members to pray for something specific. It might be "that Christ will be glorified at the funeral service;" "that the family will find a supernatural peace in the Lord;" "that the church body will be a true comfort to the family." Remember: this is not a time just to announce the death or to gossip.

Prepare for Children

Will young children be coming to the funeral? Does the family need a porta-crib, high chairs, and toys? Use the church's resources to find equipment or baby-sitters.

Because our church is bursting at the seams with young children, there's an abundance of supplies, toys, and clothing for any need. Families are ready to care for children at a moment's notice and a long list of reliable babysitters is available who are willing to care for visiting children. See if you can be instrumental in organizing this kind of network in your fellowship group.

Children often sense the tension of a crisis and need special attention and love. Offer to babysit and be creative with your care of them. Depending on their age, children would enjoy a trip to the ice cream parlor, the park, or maybe a pizza outing with other children.

Watch for special needs that arise. Offer to bathe the children and wash or set their hair before the service. For their emotional security, though, children should be with their parents at bedtime.

Do Needed Housework

In the days following a death, many people will be visiting the bereaved family. See that some of the everyday household tasks are done, such as cleaning the bathrooms, making sure there is toilet paper, changing the sheets on the beds, vacuuming the floors, doing the laundry, and watering the plants. It will be comforting to know that when Aunt Edith arrives, she'll be sleeping on clean sheets.

In an effort to help her friend, Joyce brought her cleaning lady to tidy her friend's house before the family started arriving. When she got there, Joyce realized that due to the deceased's lengthy illness, many things had not been cleaned in weeks. Joyce decided to stay and work with the cleaning lady to ready everything for company.

Check on Clothing

Has your friend decided what she'll wear to the funeral? Does it need to be dry cleaned? Does she have pantyhose without runs? Do her husband's shoes need polishing?

As Jim was dressing for the funeral, he realized the shirt he always wore with that suit was still in the ironing pile. That was one more last minute tension the family didn't need.

Process the Obituary

In times of stress, some people can't write a simple sentence. They'd appreciate your help in preparing the obituary. Be sure to include some special aspects of the person's life, checking to make sure that what you've written is accurate. Phone it in or deliver it to the appropriate papers, including any out-of-town papers that should carry the notice.

Meet Unique Needs

My friend Linda's baby was three weeks old when Linda's mother died. As a nursing mother, Linda was extremely grateful when a girl she barely knew came to the door and presented her with some frozen breast milk. "I pumped this in case you get low, or in case you have to leave your baby. Put it in the freezer. It defrosts very quickly."

Linda said, "What meant even more than the milk was that somebody understood some of my concerns and took time to meet them. I have a special feeling for her, even though we were not close friends."

Provide Special Touches

When my husband's mother died, we decided to have a picture of her at the memorial service in place of a casket. I suggested that we use one taken at our wedding which was such a special day for us all.

We had it enlarged and displayed, surrounded by flowers, at the altar. Later, I used that picture as a first page in a memorial scrapbook. In it I put all the sympathy cards, floral cards and messages we received. It clearly represents the love others expressed toward us at the time of our loss. And since they never had the opportunity to know her, it will help my children understand what their grandmother was like.

Another idea springs from a special touch my mother provided the day I came home after losing my baby. Giving me a scrapbook, she said, "It's so easy to remember the negative things and keep a record of wrongs. Use this book to keep a record of rights. Put down all the thoughtful things people are doing for you, such as bringing meals, watching Randy, Jr., sending flowers, calling to say they're praying for you and writing you cards." That book was a reminder of the light that shone in my darkness.

Is there something in the house painful for the family to look at, such as pictures or personal belongings? Ask if they'd like you to put the things away. If they would, write down where you put the items so they can find them later. Ask if there's a special remembrance they'd like to have on display, such as a family Bible, a baby picture or a special trophy.

Most importantly, take time to quiet the family and have prayer with them. Nothing calms the heart like a few moments before God. They may not be able to pray for themselves, but you can express their burdens, sorrow and faith to Him for them.

9

Help with the Funeral

Why are funerals so difficult for us to attend? One reason is because they remind us of our own vulnerability. In addition, we don't know what to do. The following suggestions may help us relax and give us the confidence we need to minister.

Making Arrangements

Before the funeral, make yourself available to help the family prepare for the service. See if they'd like you, or someone else, to go with them to the funeral home to make final arrangements or to the cemetery to pick out a plot. They'll want to make those decisions themselves, but having a friend that can be objective may be very helpful.

73

At the Funeral Home

The family may set up a visitation time at the funeral home when friends can bring flowers, pay their final respects to the deceased, and sign the guest book. It usually occurs the night before the service and can be anytime from noon through 9 P.M. Call to find out whether there will be a visitation time, or look for a listing of the hours in the newspaper.

Probably those closest to the deceased will choose to have a private time there. So don't expect to see them. But that doesn't mean it isn't important for you to go. When they see your flowers or name in the guest book, they'll be touched to know that you cared enough to come to the visitation.

If the family is present when you visit, that means they want to be with you and want you to share their loss. Identify yourself and your relationship with the deceased and share some of your personal feelings with the family. Even if the family has chosen cremation, there may be visitation hours. Call the funeral home to find out. It is appropriate for you to visit the funeral home in that case as well.

If there is no public visitation time, it is thoughtful to stop by the family home. Call first to see when is a good time. Doing nothing is often seen as a lack of concern.

The Funeral

Be sure to arrive promptly at the services so you'll have enough time to quiet your heart. As you sit there, think about the deceased, and deal with your own feelings of loss. Remember what the person meant to you, the impact he had on your life, the ways God used him to minister to you, the particular times you will miss him.

Express your own grief to the Lord. As you are praying, ask God to reveal what you can do to assist family members during this time. Commit yourself to share their burdens and provide the comfort they need.

Be sure to sign the guest book. At such a stressful time, the family may not remember who attended, but they'll use that guest list after the funeral to remind them and thank God for the love each person showed.

When the funeral ends, you'll probably be dismissed by rows to walk by the family area. If they're behind a curtain or divider, look toward them to express your sympathy; if they're seated out in the front section, be sure to greet them.

At a recent funeral, the family was seated in the front row and as we passed by, we stopped to greet them. Because they were seated, it was very difficult to give them a hug. But we reached out quietly to them and held their hand, or leaned down to offer our strength with a hug. You may not be able to express your feelings in words, but your mere presence will be a comfort.

Do you plan to be at the house following the service? Tell them so. If not, let them know a specific time when you will see them in the near future. Whatever arrangements you make, be sure they know they can count on your tangible support. I find it easier to know what to say if I have something concrete in mind to do for them.

If there's a dinner afterward and you've come a long way, plan to stay. In any event, never leave without making some kind of contact with the family. When and how to do so will depend on the format of the service and whether or not the family is available. Don't think just because there seem to be closer friends around that the bereaved do not need to see you.

Other family members whom you don't know may be present. Introduce yourself and tell how you knew their loved one. Did you work together, go to school together? Were you in the same Bible study with them?

When the time is right, share some special things you can remember about the deceased—some warm experience you've had that they may not even know. You'll give them positive things to consider and remember concerning their loved one.

Apply these suggestions to the next situation involving loss that you must face and you'll have a greater understanding of what the family is experiencing and a deeper peace about attending the service.

Take Family Pictures

Unfortunately, a funeral is one of the few times that the whole family is together for a family portrait. You can help by locating an experienced photographer to take the pictures.

Vicky told me how difficult this was to do immediately after her brother died. Because they wanted him represented in the pictures, one of the small grandchildren held his basketball for the portrait.

Disperse Personal Belongings

Although this isn't always necessary, if some of the deceased's belongings will be passed on to family that is visiting, your offer to help disperse them could be a welcome relief. It's very painful for the family to go through the belongings. But it's a necessary step in dealing with the reality of the death. Be very careful to handle this delicately, and only if the family wants your help.

When my husband's grandmother passed away, he traveled to the Midwest for the funeral. During his visit, he went to the family home and packed up things that had been designated for him so he could take them home when he left.

On the other hand, don't rush the bereaved into giving away personal belongings before they're ready to face that very emotional step.

Judy told me that after her stepfather's funeral, she and her mother went to the cemetery and distributed some of the flowers to local hospitals. When they returned home, they discovered that her stepbrothers had torn up the house, packing up things that had belonged to her stepfather and would have eventually been passed on to them.

Keep Records

The bereaved won't be able to remember every detail surrounding the funeral, but those memories will be important later. So make sure that there are notepads and pens near each phone on which messages can be recorded to be reviewed in the future. Have a guest book at the home for visitors to sign.

Other things you can do include:

Save the local newspaper from the day of the death.

Clip the obituary notices from other papers.

Accompany the family to their safe deposit box and record the information that is kept there for the family.

Chris told me about a family whose son had died. She arrived shortly afterward and found the family so distraught that they couldn't make necessary arrangements. She'd worried all the way over about what she'd say when she got there, but she soon realized that she didn't have to say much. Just giving family members a hug and telling them how sorry she was and how much she liked their son was enough.

After that, she did things to meet their physical needs. In the midst of their crisis, she had food on the table at meal time, washed the dishes, and arranged for meals to be brought in.

Since the family hadn't started to make their phone calls, Chris asked whom they wanted notified. When they couldn't decide, with their permission, she began going through their phone list. She called their friends and let them know about John's death, the time of the funeral, and encouraged them to visit the family.

Chris said she was there from 8 A.M. until midnight for four days helping to meet the family's physical needs. During that time, she called the pastor and led her friends through the funeral arrangements. When it was over, the family told her thankfully, "We could never repay you for all you've done for us."

Chris responded, "Next time you have a friend in need, go to them and do the same thing. That's all the payment I want."

You can't follow every suggestion I've listed. Be sensitive and willing to help and you'll discern which needs you can meet. Use your talents, but do not put yourself under pressure to perform a task that is undesirable to you. Instead, do the things that you enjoy naturally. But remember, you are an extension of Christ. He wants to use you to meet the bereaved's physical and emotional needs at this time.

What You Can Say....

The following suggestions are not word-for-word statements to make, but rather a reflection of a heart attitude you should have in reaching out to your hurting person. May God fill you with His tenderness and compassion enabling you to be an extension of His love.

	DO SAY	DON'T SAY
At a funeral	I'll always remember.... I'll come by with dinner tonight.	He's so much better off in heaven. If there's anything I can do, call.
A baby died	I know how much being a mother means to you.	You can always have another one. Be thankful you have Jenny. At least you never got to know it.
Divorce	The future must seem frightening. I'll stay close. I'm sure this is a lonely time for you— let's have lunch.	I never liked the way he treated you. There are two sides to every story.

Legal crisis	It's not important what happened. I just want you to know that I care.	Will you lose everything? Tell me how it happened.
Handicapped child	She has beautiful eyes. She is so loving and precious.	What are you going to do with her? If you'd taken better care of yourself, this wouldn't have happened.
Elderly parent	I know how much you love her, I'm sure you're doing the right thing.	How could you put your own mother in such a place?
Loss of home	I've been a part of some very beautiful memories here.	Remember our home is really in heaven.
Friend moving	I've seen what special friends you are. I know you'll miss each other.	Well, you can always write.
Pet dies	I know she was important to your family. Sometimes this brings back other sad feelings.	It's only a dog! You can always buy a new kitten.
During terminal illness	How are you feeling about what you are facing? I'll take you to your next doctor's appointment.	I know a lady who had the same thing. . . . Won't you be glad to be with the Lord?

	DO SAY	DON'T SAY
After death of terminally ill	Even though he needed a lot of your time, I know you'll miss his company.	It must be such a relief now that it's over.
Death of a spouse	I know how much he meant to you, and how you'll miss him.	You were so lucky to have him for 30 years.
Loss of a body part	I'm sure this will take a lot of adjustment. I'll be with you every step of the way.	At least you still have your mind. Be glad it wasn't worse.

10

Picking out a Card

When you don't know what to say, send a card or note. Unless they're close friends, that's the best way to acknowledge a person's pain and initiate comfort. Additionally, it gives you the opportunity to think through what you want to say to your hurting person.

Finding just the right card isn't easy, however. Johnny Cash was asked why his music is so different from most other country and western singers. He replied, "You can tell most of them have never walked in the woods."

Many of the messages on the cards through which I've searched the last few years sounded the same way. They don't show real understanding. They suggest that grieving persons find peace in the future, but they don't address their present anguish.

Fortunately, there are a few lines of cards that do express the sensitivity that is important. One company,

Heart to Heart, produces cards that "make it easy to communicate supportive, caring feelings during special life experiences." *These people really know how to comfort the hurting,* I thought when I first read them.

My favorite says outside, "I'd like to wrap you up in love." Inside it goes on, "and take the hurt away." Isn't that just what you've wanted to say to an acquaintance who's experienced a loss? Versatile, this card can be used for many different situations and sums up hard to express feelings.

Another in that line says, "When you hurt...I hurt too." Wouldn't you like to receive a card like that when you are facing a crisis?

"I know you are going through a rough time," a third reads, expressing similar sentiments. All three of these cards acknowledge that there is a loss and offers your love and support. This is the first step we need to take in order to comfort our friends.

When We Don't Understand

I found a card that clearly addresses the fact that many disturbing events happen in people's lives for which we have no explanation. It says, "It must be hard to understand...I don't understand either, but I love you." When someone dies in an accident, is diagnosed as having a complex disorder, has lost a job for no apparent reason, or is going through some other Job-like experience, this is a good one to send.

Suppose someone you know is having a hard time understanding why they can't get over what seems to be a minor loss, like a pet's death, a miscarriage, or a friend moving away. Heart to Heart has a card that accurately explains such strong reactions. "All that we love deeply becomes a part of us."

Another card emphasizes God's unconditional love and acceptance. "He comes to us where we live...He loves us as we are." As friends, we need to express that kind of love and communicate the fact that, no matter what situation they are experiencing, God is with them and accepts them where they are. And we do also.

Two other cards are more general, but they still offer support. One says, "You are in my thoughts...and heart." The second, "I'm praying for you today...and tomorrow too!" Knowing you are thinking and praying will uplift your hurting person and bring her comfort in what otherwise could be a sad or lonely day.

Roserich Designs, producers of Flavia cards, has several cards that express understanding. One says, "The words we most want to say are difficult to find sometimes. Their journey begins far, far away in the heart."* We do want to communicate the feelings of our heart to comfort our friends, and we know that words can never take away or minimize someone's loss. To do that, we need to provide ourselves as a supporter.

Many have told me that they felt their friends wanted them to be strong and not cry in their time of grief. A Flavia card I send frequently very delicately allows for tears. "To let you know I care, and wish I could soothe the empty place inside your heart where tears are born."* This expresses your concern and inability to take away the hurt or fill the empty place, but also lets the bereaved know that tears are a very natural response to that empty place.

Another message communicates that you have an accepting heart and are willing to help. "If you ever hurt or need someone to talk to—please know I'm here and my heart will listen."* A grieving person probably wouldn't call and say, "I hurt and need to talk to you."

But we can send a card that lets her know we're available.

If the opportunity does come to do that, spend time with her and provide leads in the conversation that will encourage her to talk and share her concerns. And make sure you're listening with your heart.

An ideal card to send to someone you can't be with physically is part of another line called, "A Time of Life on Cottage St." (Roserich Designs). Outside, a little boy in a wagon is looking off into the stars. Inside it says, "I wish I could be with you and hold your hand."* You might add, "But please know that my heart and prayers are with you during this difficult time."

Another of their cards has many uses, but is particularly helpful when words are inadequate and support is essential. On the front a young girl is holding some flowers. Inside it says, "I can't find the words to say how I feel. I'm here if you need me."*

A third that I think is lovely and honest has a cover picturing an apron-clad woman trying to select some flowers. Inside it says, "I wish I could make the hurt go away."*

Cards by Blue Mountain Arts also express the sensitivity and compassion that is essential in comforting. Each one I've found communicates true friendship, no matter what the circumstances, and states your availability and willingness to share the other person's sorrow.

I'm not suggesting that these are the only cards to send, but they are an example of the kind that expresses the appropriate emotions to your hurting friends. Before you can really minister to their needs, you must acknowledge their hurt, and tell them in your card or note that you care, support them, share their anguish, are praying for them, and love them unconditionally.

Helpful Books

Blue Mountain Arts also produces a small book of poems titled, *Life Isn't Always Easy, But Always Know That I Care.* These are the feelings we need to offer our suffering friend.

Chuck Swindoll's book, *For Those Who Hurt,* has ministered to me over and over again. Because I'm an emotional person, it helped me to read, "When words fail, tears flow. Tears have a language all their own, a tongue that needs no interpreter."

His quotation from Psalm 56 was so comforting. David says, "The Lord has heard the voice of my weeping" (v. 8). I often include some of the thoughts from this section when I send a sympathy card. They release the bereaved to express their sorrow and tears, and remind them that God hears our weeping.

Recently I discovered a little booklet by Amy Ross Mumford, *It Hurts to Lose a Special Person.* As the title suggests, it's a good one to send someone close to you. In it, the author suggests that it's okay to hurt and feel sad at the loss of a loved one. She goes on to offer hope, looking ahead to future fulfillment. This is a beautiful gift for someone who's recently lost a special person.

What to Say in Your Note

The card you send is very important and will serve as a demonstration of your love and support. The person to whom you send it will probably read and reread it many times for years to come. While its printed message will minister, so will the personal note you add.

My grandmother passed away last month, and I received many touching cards. One friend wrote, "I have always admired you for the caring and patience you have shown in taking care of your grandmother. I'm sure being a part of your home enriched her life.'' It was special to know that my friend saw the effort it took to have Grammy with us, but also knew the special relationship we had.

Another friend wrote, ''Having lost my grandma, I can relate to the loss you are feeling. No one can take the place of a dear Grandma!'' If you have shared a similar experience with the person you're writing, tell them in your note.

Expressing those same feelings, a colleague wrote, ''I share your loss as a few years ago, Ron and I walked a similar path.'' That's all you need to say. They don't need to hear all the minute details of your tragedy; but it is helpful to know that another person has faced a similar time in their life.

Another thought to include is what the individual meant to you. One mother in our church wrote, ''Grammy was always cheerful and interested in my baby Jacob. I will remember her fondly. Grammas are such precious gifts. (I still miss mine after 14 years.)''

When sending a sympathy card add a note about what the surviving relative meant to the deceased. My grandmother's sister wrote me a letter shortly after Grammy's death and said, ''Thanks to you for being such a caring granddaughter to her. She said so many times you were the one person who seemed to care what happened to her. Needless to say there were many others, but you had the knack of letting her know your feelings.'' That comment from my great aunt made all my efforts on Grammy's behalf worthwhile. What a blessing a few sentences can be to an aching heart.

If you are writing to people that you don't know well, be sure to identify yourself and tell them how you knew their loved one. Share a special quality that you admired about the deceased, an impact they made in your life, or an interesting experience you shared with them. Let the family know that you share their loss and that you will miss them also.

Remember to address the card to the whole family. Many of the cards I received after Grammy's death were addressed solely to me, even though my husband and children loved her as well. And send cards to others besides the immediate family. Recently a friend of my mother's died. Mother received many cards from other friends expressing their sympathy and acknowledging the loss mother was feeling.

Sending cards, notes, or letters is a good way to make initial contact with someone enduring a crisis, but it is important to remember that the comforting shouldn't stop there. Keep sending little notes or cards to brighten their day. Let them know how often you are thinking of them—what you are asking God to do for them.

Send cards that you would like to receive if you were in a similar situation. Many people have sent me cards I've appreciated, expressing their love and support. That has encouraged me to use similar ideas to comfort others.

11

Long-Term Help

I Shouldn't Be Here

This isn't where I'm supposed to be,
The things that are happening shouldn't
  be happening to me.
Other things were planned for, hoped for,
  and dreamed of.
This time was going to be full of so much
  light and love.
But that hasn't happened—it hasn't been able
  to be,
And so—"I shouldn't be here" is all my mind
  can see.

Gladys Chmiel

"Friends and relatives who listen, console, and react

with understanding, are cherished by those who are
hurting. Existing relationships may be strengthened
when there is a deepened appreciation of another's af-
fection and helpfulness. New friendships may develop
with people who were not previously close, but who
provided a special word or action at the right moment.
Those who realize that the need for support lasts a long
time, and who are there to offer it, are the ones who
help make it possible for the bereaved to go on."[3]

As the shock of any major crisis begins to wear off,
reality sets in. With the reality comes depression and
emotional turmoil. This is when your hurting person
is apt to say, "I shouldn't be here" or "I'm not supposed to be doing this." Other things were planned for
this time in their life:

- The widow had a retirement with her husband planned.
- Expectant parents of a stillborn were
  joyously awaiting the birth of their child.
- A newly-divorced woman had always expected to live "happily ever after."
- A highly-respected family is faced with
  public humiliation following a legal crisis.
- Parents hoping to have their children nearby find their serviceman son transferred to
  the Philippines. About that time, their
  daughter leaves for a college on the other
  side of the United States.
- A young couple is told that the baby
  they've been waiting to adopt for five years
  is finally available, only to learn that the
  birthing mother has changed her mind.
- A husband who has been with a company
  for five years is called into the manager's

office and told that his services are no
longer needed. Two months later he is still
without work and has depleted their sav-
ings.

All of these situations have long-term implications.
A person experiencing any of them will need your continued support.

Usually, at the onset of an obvious crisis, the church
family jumps in to help meet the immediate needs. But
long-term needs often go ignored. That's because the
urgency is gone, their friends' lives have returned to
normal, and they assume that the hurting person must
be doing the same thing. Unfortunately that's just when
the depth of the loss or its severity is coming into full
view. From that point on is when the hurting person
needs your understanding and comfort more than ever.

The Road Back

Our timetable for the hurting is often unrealistic.
They should put the past behind them and get on with
their lives—especially if it is taking longer for them to
get over their hurting than we think it should.

It's important to realize that a significant change has
occurred that will leave a permanent imprint in the
bereaved's life. Never try to minimize the significance
of the crisis. Instead, allow individuals to grieve normally and appropriately, and provide them with the
essential support they need. Given enough time and
support most people make their way through the painful stages of grief and regain their emotional balance.

In the meantime, they need friends who will allow
them to hurt in their own way, at their own pace and
who will not insist that they act like their old selves.

No one who has suffered a terrible crisis will ever be her old self again. She may be a different self, or even a better self, but she will never be the same person she was before her life was touched by trauma.

Ways to Include Them

When there has been a death or divorce, those affected will need continued, special attention. Often the families feel left out and ignored. So, whenever it's natural to do so, include them in as many of your activities as possible.

Take them to lunch, invite them shopping or to the movies, have them over for dinner, spend the day sorting through things at their house.

Caution: some things will be too difficult for them to do too soon. They cannot avoid all painful experiences, but sometimes they will know ahead of time that they're not ready for a particular experience yet.

For parents who have lost their baby, a friend's baby shower might be too hard to attend. For a widow, a couple's holiday party full of fun and fellowship could be too painful. When a teenage child has died, attending the local graduation ceremonies or school basketball game would only point to their own loss. As time goes by, they'll need to face various types of pain, but they'll need to do so gradually and with your understanding and support.

Holiday Help

Anniversaries of certain events are apt to be very difficult times for the bereaved, such as birthdays, due dates, wedding anniversaries, or holidays. Be sure to call your friend at these times and say, "I know this is your son's birthday and I wanted you to know that I have been praying for you. How are you feeling today?"

By acknowledging that this could be a difficult day for him, you are giving him an opportunity to talk and allowing him the freedom to admit, "Yes, it is a rough time." On the other hand, he may not want to talk about it. Maybe it isn't a problem that day. Either way, he'll be touched that you cared enough to remember him at a potentially difficult time.

Long-Term Prayer

Commit yourself to pray for your hurting friends daily and let them know that you are doing it. Ask what specific areas they'd like you to pray about. Often a deeply hurting person is unable to pray for himself and will be blessed to know that you're praying.

Continue to ask God to show you his needs and how you can minister to him, so that you can be His instrument of comfort. And before you call or visit your friend, pray and ask God to guide your time together, so you'll be the encouragement your friend needs.

Encourage Them to Reach Out

As time passes and your friend begins to surface from the depth of his loss, encourage him to reach out to help others. Some will be able to build relationships with others who've suffered in a similar fashion. They only need to be one step ahead in the grief process to help someone else.

Others can serve as role models, showing that it's possible to experience a loss and get through it. One of the most effective ways of getting over our own hurts is helping others with theirs.

Divorce

The devastation of a divorce may take years to resolve. Your friend will need continued, non-judgmental support. Each step that must be taken requires a new grief process. We must first acknowledge the new need, support them through that step, and help them come to a resolution of that need. Inevitably, as soon as one aspect is dealt with and your friend is beginning to adjust, new problems surface and the process starts all over.

As with a death, anniversaries, holidays, and birthdays can be very painful times for your divorced friend and she needs your love. Let her know you're aware that this might be a difficult time and that you are available whenever she needs you. Invite her to join you for dinner or a movie on one of those dates. Some kind of a positive diversion can be very helpful. Identify the potentially painful time and offer your concern, and you'll be a real comfort to your friend.

There are many legal technicalities with a divorce, accompanied by multiple court appearances. Make sure that your friend has someone accompanying her to court, that the children are cared for, and that meals are provided. These are very emotionally draining times and your friend needs continued help. Before each court appearance, let your friend know that you have been praying for her. Offer to pray with her now.

Continually acknowledge that you know how difficult this is for her and that you will be with her throughout whatever lies ahead. Keep an open heart and listen to her concerns without being judgmental.

Be creative in meeting this family's special needs. For example, suppose a major change in the family structure has taken place. Help minimize the void that has been created by including them in your activities. Keep in mind that one parent is now carrying the full responsibility of running the household. She'll need support and time out from the daily routine.

Legal Crises

During any kind of legal crisis, a family needs unconditional love and support. Few people know the detailed explanations of the problem. It's easy to make hasty assessments and offer advice. The last thing the family needs is a judgment of innocence or guilt. We're not called to be God's earthly judges. Even if there is some element of guilt or responsibility involved, it's not our job to chastise our friends.

What they do need is continued prayer and support. God has shown us total forgiveness and we are no better than any other human, regardless of their actions. So demonstrate God's unconditional love to your friends. They'll be experiencing the same grief process as in any other crisis. They need you to acknowledge that they have a need, that you will support them through the process and be with them to its conclusion—which could take years. Regardless of their innocence or guilt, they need you to be God's instrument of comfort.

Whether the problem is unemployment, divorce, death, loneliness or any other crisis, your friends need your prayers, presence, participation, and support on a long-term basis. The more you understand what they're going through, the more you can help.

The next five chapters are designed to do that. Each tells one person's story of a crisis through which he lived, how he felt, and how others helped (and failed to help) him cope.

12

The Loss of a Child

It has been 10 years since the day Beverly's baby died, yet she still remembers it as if it were yesterday. "I always wanted a large family and was thrilled to learn I was pregnant again." Her three boys, age seven, five and two shared her excitement at the prospect of a new baby in the house. "Would we have another boy? Or would we have a girl?"

When she suffered a miscarriage at three months, she was heartsick. She'd never had any complications with her previous pregnancies, and kept asking herself what went wrong. "Was it because there had been something wrong with my baby? I became pregnant again very easily. This time I found myself wondering if something was wrong. What would I do if something happened to this child?" Despite her concerns, the pregnancy continued with no complications.

One evening after dinner, she was resting in the living room with the family when she felt the baby bounce around so much that her dress moved. "That baby sure is a strong one!" her husband said, grinning.

A few hours later, Beverly went into labor.

Fear Becomes Reality

About midnight, they went to the hospital. When a nurse attached a fetal monitor and couldn't find a heartbeat, Beverly asked frantically, "What's wrong? What's the matter?"

"Nothing, nothing at all. Everything's just fine."

Just before the nurse walked out of the room, Beverly said, "But I don't hear a heartbeat." "Oh, you just don't know what to listen for." Right outside the door she made a phone call to Beverly's doctor. "You'd better get over here right away." The next few minutes seemed like an eternity as Beverly waited for her physician to get there.

The doctor arrived and began the examination, but he couldn't find a heartbeat either. She kept pleading with him, "Is my baby dead?" He told her that based on the indications, that certainly was a possibility.

Her contractions grew stronger and longer, but still no heartbeat. "It seemed that my fears were becoming reality. The baby had died. That morning in the doctor's office everything was fine. The heartbeat was clear, the baby was moving a lot. Every other indication was normal. What went wrong?"

The time came to enter the delivery room, and her anxiety grew with each contraction. Everything was silent. No anticipation. No joy.

Finally, her baby was born. A girl, the infant was placed on a nearby table where she lay motionless.

"I can remember those agonizing moments as if I were in the delivery room right now. The baby had strangled to death on the umbilical cord, I was told. I recounted the movement I had felt only hours before, and it was concluded that my daughter must have been strangling at that time."

Facing Death

The reality of her daughter's death began to set in when it was time to call family and friends, who were anxiously awaiting the good news, and tell them of the loss. Their pastor told Beverly's mother in person. "She took it so hard that I felt I had to be strong. But all through that time the strongest feeling I had was emptiness. Until hours ago, I had been so full of life. I felt like a vase that had been dumped out," Beverly said.

Because Beverly felt that she had to be strong and brave, and knew she'd be seeing other babies and had to get used to it, she decided to go to the nursery and look at the newborns.

All by herself, she looked into the room. When she saw one little baby crying, "My heart ached. I fell apart and could barely make it back to my room. When the nurse realized how upset I was she gave me a sedative and it seemed I slept the day away. Sleeping made it a little less painful."

One of the most devastating parts of her whole experience was leaving the hospital. Because she'd been overdue with all her babies and had had many false alarms, when she'd left for the hospital this time, her mom had called out, "Don't come home empty-handed."

"How those words came back to haunt me! I *was* leaving 'empty-handed.' My arms literally ached for the baby that was supposed to be there." Instead of celebrating the birth of a new life, Beverly had to make funeral plans, choose a casket, and grave site. "I wasn't supposed to be doing this now. This was supposed to be a time of joy and celebration, not a time of death and sorrow." Her minister offered her a ray of sunshine when he reminded her that she had a deposit waiting in heaven.

Because she'd always thought that if she ever had a little girl, she'd dress her in ruffled dresses with bows in her hair, that's the way she dressed her baby for the funeral.

"We did have a daughter. We just didn't get to raise her. She's very special to us and we felt it was important that she have a name. After much prayer it was decided to give her the name we had chosen for a girl during our first pregnancy. Her name is Megan."

How Some Helped

A friend who'd recently lost a child to crib death was at the funeral home and took pictures of Megan. The last picture he took was of the sunset that evening. Later he put the pictures in an album. When he showed the couple the sunset with its gorgeous pink and blues he said, "This is the sky the night of Megan's funeral. This is where your daughter and my son are."

Those pictures have become precious because they're the only real remembrance Beverly has of Megan. "She is very real to me. She is my daughter."

People did many other things to help during that time. While she was still hospitalized she asked her husband to dismantle the crib, pack up all the baby clothes, and put them away. When she realized that he was hurting too, and that it wasn't fair to ask him to go through that alone, she changed her mind. "Let's wait until I get home."

She was thankful when a dear friend came over and helped her put the things away. "It was very difficult for me, but I clung to the hope that maybe they wouldn't have to be packed away too long."

A note her grandmother sent was very special and comforting. ["She said that she could understand how sad I must be feeling and that she would be praying for me everyday.] When my grandmother says she's going to pray, you know she is going to pray. Her understanding and warmth was very comforting."

Early Stages of Grief

After the funeral Beverly knew she had to start on the road to recovery, but instead she tended to pity herself and get depressed. "I'd go into the bedroom and sit on the floor and cry." The more she dwelled on her baby's death, the more depressed she got. With three other children who depended on and needed her, she knew she had to be strong.

Hindrances

But she wasn't prepared for the thoughtless comments people made following her daughter's death. "I'm sure it wouldn't have been so bad if it was a boy you had lost. After all, you already have three boys."

"It's probably for the best, she might have been retarded."

One lady told her, "Just think, she might have turned out to be a prostitute!"

Another called and said, "If you hadn't washed the

windows that day and raised your arms you wouldn't have strangled your baby to death."

Others suggested she should sue her doctor. "I'd never go back to him!"

A friend asked, "Why didn't you go to the hospital sooner?"

Her doctor reassured her that there was nothing she could have done to prevent Megan's death, and certainly nothing she did had caused it.

Trying to comfort her, people said, "I know just how you feel." *How could they?* she asked herself. They had never had their baby die. They couldn't possibly understand what she was feeling. She got tired of hearing everybody's horror stories too. "People would call me up and tell me about their second cousin's mother-in-law who had a similar problem. I know it was an attempt to comfort me, but they weren't interested in listening to what I was feeling."

Beverly wanted so much to have someone who'd been through the same experience come and offer their support and understanding. How had someone else handled this kind of loss? Was what she was feeling normal?

She dreamed about Megan often—about her experiences in the hospital and about the funeral. "I thought those dreams would never go away." But as time went on, they diminished. Now she almost never has one.

Everytime she met someone who hadn't heard about the baby's death, she hurt all over again. "One day I was in the grocery store and a lady rushed up to me. 'I see you've had your baby. Did you have another boy?' I was hurt and she was embarrassed as I had to tell her about Megan's death."

"Another time I had to take a pair of shoes to be

repaired and the clerk said, 'Weren't you pregnant the last time you were in?'

" 'Yes, I was, but I lost the baby' was all I could manage."

Three months after Megan died, Beverly received a form letter advertising a baby product. It included the words, "May the rocking of the cradle in your home . . . ." Pain like a knife stabbed her heart. "How could the hospital have released my name as a mother with a new baby?"

The memory of the loss is eased somewhat because a dear friend remembers Megan's birthday every year and sends a card or flowers on that day. "It's such a blessing to know that someone else shares that special day with me."

Her husband was reluctant for her to get pregnant again because he was afraid to put her through another painful experience. "But the Lord was very gracious, and one year later we were blessed with another daughter."

"I did survive my losses, but they hurt! To this day, I still don't understand why they happened. I can't say that I'm happy they happened. But, I can say it strengthened my prayer life and it has made me appreciate the children I do have even more."

13

The Loss of a Home

"Mom, come quick," Barbara heard urgency in her son's voice as he yelled from the family room. She ran to him and stared in horror out the window at the mountains that surrounded their San Bernardino home. Flames crested the hill behind them and strong winds blew billows of smoke in their direction.

Because their house had a fireproof roof and was built of brick, Barbara and her family didn't think they faced a major risk of fire. Besides, news reports had indicated that the forest fire wasn't a threat to their area.

Now, with flames so close, she ran into the backyard and turned on the water. No water pressure!

Frantically, she tried to figure out what to do. *This is like a nightmare. It can't be happening to me,* she thought.

Then she remembered that people had been saved

from smoke inhalation during the MGM Grand Hotel fire by putting wet towels over their faces. Running back through the bedroom, she grabbed her husband's handkerchiefs, wet them and threw one to her son, another to her husband's secretary and kept one for herself.

By this time, flames had reached their backyard. "Get out! We've got to get out! We can't save it," Barbara yelled to the others. They tied handkerchiefs around their faces, while she got the pets in the car and turned the horse loose. Barbara grabbed her purse and keys and they raced to the car.

"Everything was frantic," she remembers. "I kept worrying, 'Will we get out in time?' " As they drove out the driveway, she looked back and saw flames near the house. It looked as if it were catching fire underneath the eaves. *The house would not be saved.* She knew that now. There would be no miracle. A minute later, a huge fireball hit the house and it exploded.

Her initial feeling was one of desperation. "I can't take this. After everything else that has happened in my life I can't handle this. I'm sure the fact that my father deserted us when I was a child and that I had almost died as a result of a tragic accident just a few years before, compounded my feelings of helplessness."

"I remember asking God, 'Why? You could have saved our house. It's not fair.' " Some houses were spared, although 295 other families did lose their homes in that fire.

Barbara and her family moved in with some thoughtful friends who invited them for a few days until they could make more permanent arrangements. The next morning they returned to find the property nothing but a smoldering heap. Underneath the rubble, the cement was still hot and embers glowed. All that was left standing was part of the fireplace and chimney. Absolutely nothing could be salvaged.

Letting Go

Everything Barbara owned had been destroyed. The family literally had nothing but the clothes on their backs.

"I had to face the fact that all my possessions were gone. I had to let them go. There were family heirlooms and personal things that meant so much to me. I knew if I didn't release them, I'd become a bitter woman, mourning after the pretty things I'd owned and was sentimentally attached to." But she felt as though she wouldn't be able to stand the heartbreak.

Facing Facts

Barbara was in a state of shock and inertia when her friend, Linda, called and said she'd go buy the family some clothes if Barbara would just write down the sizes they wore. But Barbara hadn't even begun when Linda arrived. "I hadn't even thought about what we needed, let alone the sizes. I remember stalling. 'I don't know what we do need.' "

"Barbara, I know you'll need some cosmetics, underwear, shoes, nightgowns and much more. I want to help you."

The two women went to a department store to shop. There, among the racks of clothes, reality suddenly hit Barbara. *I don't even own a single nightgown.* Totally overwhelmed, she sat in a chair in the shoe department and waited while Linda shopped throughout the store, gathering the essentials the family needed.

"I was so thankful to have a friend who cared enough about us to shop for me and start me thinking about the future."

Thanksgiving Day, which came not long after the fire, began as a solemn occasion. But as Barbara and her family sat around the dinner table at her mother's house, she began to realize how much she did have to be thankful for. "We didn't have a house, but we did have each other. No one had been hurt in the fire. We still had the components to make a home again. We were healthy and our two teenaged children knew they had parents who loved them."

Friends Help

After the remains cooled, a crew of friends arrived to help clear the debris. Just when the crew was getting hungry, a woman Barbara had only met once pulled in the driveway and dropped down the back of her station wagon. "Here's lunch." She'd cooked several huge casseroles of lasagna, made garlic bread and a salad. She had food enough for everyone.

All day, while bulldozer, tractor, and two dumptrucks worked, Barbara could only stand by in a daze, visiting with friends who stopped by, and watch the debris of her home piled into trucks and hauled away. It took 13 loads.

The next day about noon, one of the men who'd returned to finish the job went to McDonald's and came back with hamburgers, fries and drinks. "I appreciated the fact that I didn't have to worry about the food. He'd seen a need and taken the initiative to fill it. There was no hassle over 'Who wants what?' or 'Who owes what?' " she said.

As word got out about the fire, bags of clothing of

every kind, color and size—from fuchsia polyester pants to black mini-skirts—began arriving. Some were things people knew would fit and be used, while other things were old and worn out.

They moved into a rental home in the mountains while Barbara's husband completed the mountain cabin he was building to sell. Then they moved in and furnished it. "It seemed as though I'd just gotten settled when it was sold, and all the furniture with it. That meant starting all over again." To some, that would have been an exciting challenge; to her it meant she still had nothing she could call her own, and nowhere to call home.

That's why the "starting over" shower ladies from her church held for her was so special. "Most of the things they brought were very practical, like appliances, linens, and tableware. But it was fun to get some non-essentials like a beautiful crystal bud vase and a delicate set of stemware." More than anything, it showed how much they really cared.

Long-Term Help Needed

After they moved to the mountains, though, "it seemed as if most of our friends stopped calling. It felt as if, since we were out of sight, we were out of their minds. People were so helpful immediately following the fire, but now it seemed as though they thought their job was done."

What she desperately needed, she says, were people who'd stayed close to her and been her friends. "I appreciated those who invited us over for dinner, especially since I couldn't reciprocate."

She also needed people who understood how she felt—how terrible and overwhelming it was going to be to have to start all over again. Instead, some made comments like, "It'd be kind of fun to get to buy all new things and start fresh," or "This time you'll get a new house built from the ground up, instead of one you have to remodel." Others said, "Since John is such a good builder, I'm sure you'll have a nicer house than you had before."

Barbara says, "I didn't really care about what I might have in the future. All I could think about was what we had lost."

When someone committed themselves to pray and called to see how the family was doing or what they could do to help, she was especially thankful. But if a friend called and asked, "How are you doing?" she says she knew all he wanted to hear was, "I'm doing just fine." She didn't feel free to tell those people how lonely she was, how overwhelmed by the things she had to do. "I needed people who would keep me involved, help me move, and see what they could do for me."

Barbara became most depressed when she thought about the house that had been destroyed. "I had a trunk filled with the children's baby shoes, clothes, and special things I'd saved to give them when they got married. It's still hard to believe that in 10 minutes, it was all gone.

"But I knew that I had to accept my loss. So a couple of times, I went through the house room by room in my mind and remembered what color it was, where the furniture was, where the pictures hung, and what the view was from that window.

"I reminded myself that it was lovely there, that I had beautiful memories of our lives in that house." It was the destruction of the family home that was the terrible memory, but she could hold onto all the years of good memories when her children were growing up there. That would never minimize the loss she experienced, but she was learning to face the tragedy, let it go and focus on her positive memories.

14

The Loss of Two Fathers

Carolyn's father had been in the hospital for three months when her mother awoke her one morning. "I want to talk to you before your grandmother does and makes a big production out of this." Matter-of-factly, she told Carolyn that her father had died.

He'd had cancer for several years. As a preschooler, Carolyn hadn't understood exactly what was wrong, but she knew he was different from most other fathers because he stayed in bed a lot.

My daddy is dead. He is with Jesus. I won't see him anymore, Carolyn thought.

Because she was a child, she was left out of most events following his death, but she did attend the funeral. "I couldn't figure out what was going on. My mother and brothers were crying, and when the minister insisted I look inside the casket, I wanted to crawl in there with my dad. He looked the way he had when he was lying in a hospital bed, and I'd been allowed to get on it with him and clown around." When she saw his body she figured her daddy was asleep.

Months later, when her mother was bathing her, Carolyn asked, "If Jesus loves us, how come He doesn't take the hurt away?" For the first time her mother realized that her daughter was hurting. Now Carolyn knows, that although children may not show visible signs of mourning, they do experience grief which parents need to notice.

"After he died I felt different from others because I didn't have a father. It embarrassed me, and I blamed my mother. Why did I have to go to Campfire Girls and other father-daughter events and bring my mother?"

Two girlfriends' fathers tried to provide Carolyn with the male image she needed, although they knew they couldn't compensate for the loss of her father. Both families made special efforts to include her in family activities. Carolyn gave both men gifts on Father's Day. In addition, her oldest brother tried to fill some of the void her father's death created.

A Second Father and Delayed Grief

When she was 14, Carolyn's mother remarried. Brad, who'd been a friend of her father's, told Carolyn he didn't want to take her dad's place. "But that doesn't mean we can't love each other and have a good relationship and home life," he went on.

Brad and her mother talked often about her father, and what he was like. "For three years or so, I couldn't talk about my dad without crying." Carolyn longed to see her father, to know him, to have contact with anything he'd had contacted, and to know what he stood for.

"I did the majority of my grieving during those years. I found that I had a lot of unresolved feelings, but I didn't understand and thought it was strange. And I wouldn't talk about it to anybody. I had so many questions and if's. One thought I really struggled with was 'Who would I have been if my father had lived?' I never have told my mother what my feelings were then."

Anticipatory Grief

Ten years after he married Carolyn's mother, the family was stunned to learn that Brad had massive amounts of cancer. Carolyn agonized over the thought that she might lose another father. Now married and living three hours from her parents, Carolyn went back weekends to visit.

Because she was the youngest child and had lived at home for nine years after he and her mother married, Brad felt closest to Carolyn. "We had a father-daughter relationship." She visited him every time he was hospitalized and throughout that summer.

Mid-September at 5:30 A.M., he called. "Carolyn, I want to tell you I've decided to pull the plug." His words didn't sink in at first.

He explained that he couldn't live unless there was a quality to his life. All he was able to do now was lie in bed, and even with medication, the pain was so severe, he couldn't bear it.

That's when his words began to sink in. Toward the end of the conversation, Brad told Carolyn he was entering the hospital soon where they would attempt to control his pain until death.

When Brad finished he said, "I expected you to try and change my mind."

"I can't do that. Knowing how much pain you're in, it would be selfish of me to insist you go on."

At his request Carolyn went to be with her stepfather at home before he entered the hospital.

"I can't explain how strange it is to sit with someone you know is about to die and try to think of all the things you want to say. But I had peace, because I'd expressed my love for him enough times when he was well. So I didn't feel a need to rush into words or make flowery statements. It seemed inappropriate anyway. If I hadn't lived it, it was too late to say anything."

In the hospital, Brad talked mostly about God's goodness and faithfulness. He didn't blame God, nor question, "Why are you allowing me to suffer like this?" He accepted the fact that he had a loving Savior. His attitude made the experience more bearable for everyone.

Brad's physician assured the family that Brad had made his decision with a clear mind and had chosen quality of life over length of life. By the end of the week, he slipped into a coma. Carolyn remembers driving to the hospital crying, "God, you took one dad already, now you're taking number two."

"What about my children? I'd talked with Brad about being a grandfather, and he said he was sure he could look down from heaven and love them. That was comforting, but still, it didn't seem fair."

In the middle of the night on Friday, Brad died. "We knelt and prayed, thanking God that he was with Him, and felt peaceful about his passing."

But the next morning they returned home from the hospital, where they had collected his belongings, to find the whole family present. Having everyone together for every meal—children as well as grown-ups —was an uncomfortable experience.

Preparing Children

Brad had prepared his grandchildren, ages 5 and 7, for his death and told them they wouldn't be seeing him anymore. "That was such a contrast to what I remember when my natural father died," Carolyn said. At the funeral, they looked into the casket and knew they were looking at Grandpa's body, but that he was in heaven with Jesus.

Grieving Differently

Carolyn missed Brad but because he'd been in such pain, she didn't grieve the way she might have otherwise. Additionally, she was busy helping her mother deal with her loss—letting her talk about it, be depressed, and cry when she needed to.

Comforters and Frustrations

When she returned to her own home, friends brought in meals, "I felt guilty that they were doing that for me, but it was nice to come home from work, put a casserole someone else had made into the oven, and sit down and tell myself, 'You've made it through this day. Keep going; you're going to make it.' "

Teachers at the school where she taught cleaned up her school classroom and made new decorations. They helped make the open house scheduled for the day she returned run smoothly, even though it took a lot of extra work that wasn't their responsibility. Without their help, Carolyn knows she could never have gotten ready.

One frustrating response she kept getting was, "I'm so sorry." "What was I supposed to say then? I wished they'd given me something to respond to, like "How is your mother doing?" "Is there something specific I can pray about?"

Empathy

Her biggest release was to talk to someone else who'd lost a parent at this time of their life. "I really appreciated having a friend to whom I could express my grief and have her say, 'I felt the same way.' "

"I think I'd have gotten over my natural father's loss much more quickly if someone could have said, 'What you're feeling is normal. You're okay. Let's deal with it and keep going.' That experience took me so long to deal with because I wasn't willing to dredge it all back up, experience it all again, and let it all go. Instead, I did it a piece at a time."

Days driving home from work, Carolyn found herself lonely and crying because she missed her stepdad. A year later, she still experiences those feelings. Her husband gives her the opportunity to discuss it if she wants to, but drops it if she doesn't. "I really appreciate his understanding," she says.

Helping Her Mother

For the days and months following her stepfather's death, Carolyn helped her mother clean out closets and drawers and take care of other personal details. "She needed lots of support doing the simple tasks that follow a death."

One friend helped organize the florist's cards and recorded them in the memorial book. She also helped write thank you notes.

"Mom wanted me to read each little card and letter she received. I dreaded it, but did it because it meant a lot to her. The things that mean the most aren't always big, important things. Often, it's a willingness to look at special things or listen and not judge."

Her mother did appreciate hearing people tell good, positive, funny things about Brad. But she sensed that some were afraid to talk about him at all, for fear they'd upset her.

Carolyn spent three weeks with her mother the next summer, listening to her talk, tell stories, and cry. "She relived the experience of my stepfather's passing several times. My brothers and sisters were tiring of it. 'Mom needs to pick herself up and get going,' they'd tell me. I was the only person who said 'Let her feel bad.' "

Thinking she needed to keep busy, they pushed her mother into working as a volunteer a few days a week. "She'll be fine if she just stops thinking about herself," they said. But she didn't last more than two weeks. "Pushing her before she was ready was like putting a Band-Aid on her pain," Carolyn added.

Neighbors

Neighbors have been there for Carolyn's mom. They invite her over for breakfast, make sure her lawn gets mowed, and that her car is working. They fix anything that breaks around the house. Every day, they call to make sure she's all right. Their love for her is genuine and they've put it into action. Carolyn has written them many thank you notes to express how much she appreciates them.

Church Friends

"People in Mom's church have been wonderful to

her," Carolyn says. Before Brad's death, they included the couple in activities. If they knew something would be difficult or uncomfortable for Brad, they didn't plan those events.

They've continued to include Carolyn's mom in everything they do, making no distinction because she's a widow. They've remained her mother's true friends. Some have even included her in their vacation plans.

It's been more than a year since Brad died, and Carolyn notes that her mother has made significant strides. "She's bought a new house and has leased out the farm. But she waited until she was ready to do that. I don't think she could have done anything faster than she did." And she adds, "There are still many times that are hard for her."

15

The Loss of a Mother

Linda was taking a nap while her three-week-old son Stephen slept, when the phone rang. It was her dad. "Your mom hasn't gotten home yet. Did she leave on time?"

Linda's parents were vacationing at their nearby mountain cabin so her mom could be with her after Stephen was born. Because her mom and dad were going back to their year-round home that evening, her mom had stayed to help finish the laundry and straighten the house. Mother and daughter said their goodbyes, and then she left.

"I told Dad she'd probably decided to stop at the store on the way home. 'I'm sure there's nothing to worry about.' But as I hung up the phone, a feeling of panic came over me. *Where could she be?*"

Stephen awoke, Linda nursed him and decided to call

123

her dad back. Her mother still hadn't arrived and since she'd taken their only car, her dad couldn't search for her. "I heard sirens a little while ago," he told her. She could tell he was getting nervous.

"I told Dad I'd drive up to the cabin and see if I could find Mom on the way. Maybe she had had a flat tire." As she was putting Stephen in the car seat, Linda's husband, Doug, arrived and together they drove toward the cabin.

When an ambulance roared past them her fears mounted. Almost at the cabin, they found her mother's car. It was crushed.

She'd been driving up the mountain road toward her cabin when a large truck coming downhill lost control on a curve and hit her head-on. Her body was stuck in the car, and it would be hours before they could get her out. Since her mother was unconscious and the couple couldn't assist her, a policeman told them to go up to the cabin. Rescuers would call as soon as they'd gotten her out.

Linda and Doug told her dad what had happened, and called her brother, Bill, who was about two hours away. He said he'd come right up.

After the couple had agonized for hours, the call from the police finally came. They'd gotten Linda's mother out and were airlifting her to Loma Linda University Medical Center. Doug, who went to the hospital with Linda's dad and brother, kept the rest informed about her condition. Although doctors tried massaging her heart, they told the family there really was no hope. After trying one more time, they let her go.

"From the time we came upon the accident I guess I was in shock. My legs and feet were numb. Somehow I knew Mom was going to die, that it would be a miracle from God if she were healed."

Waiting was torturous, but when Doug called with the news that her mother was dead, Linda says she was at peace. "Mom was in such bad condition, I wouldn't have wanted her to live in a coma or as a vegetable. I had joy because I knew she was with the Lord."

"The person I was most concerned about was my Dad. All I could think was that I needed to help him through all of this."

Realization

The reality and grief of her mom's death began to set in during the night when she arose to care for Stephen. As she nursed the baby at 2 A.M., she and Doug opened baby gifts that had come in the mail that day. "All I could think about as I looked at each one was, 'I'll never be able to show this to Mom.'"

All the next day Linda cried. When she went out to milk the goats she kept thinking, "Mom will never be here to sit and watch me milk them again. She always wanted to learn to milk and now she's not going to do that. Everything I did, I would say, 'Mom will never do this with me again.'" Life would never be the same.

Although it was a tough day, Linda sees it as constructive. "I got a lot of it out of my system. I thought through all the things I was not going to do with Mom ever again, at least not here. I was getting over my grieving so I could start to receive the peace that God had for me."

A Purpose

She wanted to make things as positive as possible for her dad. "I had somebody that I had to be strong for and help. He'd saved his whole life for the retirement he and Mom were going to share. A close couple, they'd planned big trips and fun together."

"I feel like half of me is gone. I might as well die too," her dad told her.

Two Kinds of Support

To assist, people brought meals and visited with the family, letting them talk about anything they needed to. "We shared our joy knowing Mom was with the Lord. Sometimes I almost felt like I was in heaven during those days. I remember that time more with joy than sorrow."

The night before the funeral, as she cared for Stephen, Linda prayed. "You know I really don't want to go to the funeral and have everybody feeling sorry for me. It's not the way I want to finish off Mom's life."

"The Lord gave me peace and let me know He'd be my strength."

The Funeral

The church was packed for the funeral and because there was a sense of joy at the service, it wasn't the negative experience Linda expected. "God had been faithful and was my strength."

After the funeral, family and close friends ate the meal others had prepared and shared and laughed together. It was a very special time of fellowship.

When it ended they returned to their homes. They'd been together for three days, and now it was time to take up their individual lives again. Linda's role as new mother helped keep her busy.

Why?

Questions haunted her for months. *Did Mom suffer? How much did she hurt? Why did this have to happen? God could have worked a miracle. Why didn't He?* At times she grieved deeply. "A year after the accident, the Lord was still helping me to work through those thoughts. Finally, I experienced peace about most of it."

"Mom was with the Lord. She was happy. God was going to give me the strength to keep going and He'd meet all the needs that Mother would have taken care of. He'd have to help me be a new mother since Mom wasn't here to do that."

The Pain of Contrast

Going from the joy of birth to the devastation of death in so short a time was difficult for Linda. Stephen did keep her occupied and the joy of being a new mother had helped ease some of the pain. Each day was a new experience as she watched him grow and smile. Even so, her heart ached because her mom wasn't there to share it.

Encouragement and Support

People did many special things to encourage Linda. The beautiful notes and cards the family received were a testimonial to the life her mom had led. Linda especially appreciated those who could share her joy that her mother was with the Lord.

She was touched by the people who called, even the ones who said, "I don't know what to say to you, but I want to make contact because I really care." Their concern ministered to her. Many friends she knew as children called even though they hadn't kept in touch. Hearing from her parents' friends meant a great deal too.

The most helpful physical act was having meals delivered. As a nursing mother, with all the funeral arrangements to make and so much to deal with emotionally, she didn't have time for food preparation. Not only were people feeding her family, but her brother's family and her dad too. "That's the only reason Dad ate because other people were preparing the meals."

Offers to babysit came in as well. Most of the time she kept Stephen with her because he was such a new baby. During the funeral and a few other times, however, friends cared for him.

While the flowers at the funeral were beautiful, the most meaningful ones were sent to her home by a friend. "I could look at them and think, 'Someone really does care about me personally.' "

Many said that they were praying for something specific. One lady told Linda, "I'm praying that you will be able to continue nursing and that your milk production will stay up through all of this." It did, and she could say, "Thank you Lord, I know you are hearing their prayers." Friends prayed that she'd have a good night's sleep. Mornings when she woke, she thought gratefully about them.

"I've been so thankful for friends who've let me talk about Mom when something reminds me of her. I feel like she is still alive. Someday I'll be in her presence when I go to be with the Lord. I still love her and she still loves me. Some people have told me that I am clinging to her and not really letting her go. But I feel she is a part of my life. She was my mother and there is no reason why I shouldn't think about her."

Friends who knew some of the special things that

Linda's mom used to do for the family are carrying them on. A neighbor who knew Linda's mom would have helped prepare a big meal after Stephen's baptism, came over and helped. Another offered to babysit at times when she knew Linda's mom would have. Doug's mom provides Halloween treats the way Linda's mom did. While no one has ever tried to replace her, they have helped fill some of the void her death created.

Many made special efforts to remember the family during the holidays, like close friends of her parents who spent Christmas with the couple. A friend sent Linda flowers for her birthday. "The thought that the one who gave birth to me wasn't going to be there to share that day was hard to take. Without speaking a word, they let me know they were thinking about me and that meant a lot."

Particularly during the first year after the loss, she really appreciated those who wrote saying they knew this was a difficult time for her. She needed to know friends hadn't forgotten and were praying for her.

"Many of Mom's close friends still keep in touch. That shows me how important Mom was to them and that they care about her children. It takes a special effort to do that and it is a blessing."

Even after six years, one friend still calls or sends a note on the day her mom died. "She always remembers Mom's birthday, too. 'Are you having a hard time right now with your Mom being gone?' she'll ask. 'I want you to know I've been praying that today wouldn't be too hard on you.' or 'I know it's almost the fifth anniversary of the accident. How are you doing?' "

"One old friend called long distance and we cried together. That was an important release for me. I was touched by the people at the funeral who hugged me and cried. I appreciated them sharing those emotions with me."

The Other Side

A few things people did were not helpful at all. Some sent sympathy cards two or three months late, even though they'd known about her death since the day it happened. It seemed to Linda as though they'd forgotten it and then remembered when they were ready to send out their Christmas cards.

"It's wonderful to continue to send notes and stay in touch, but a sympathy card should be sent right away. After a while I began to get tired of ones that kept mentioning how sorry everybody was. I was getting to the point where I needed to hear positive things instead."

Occasionally, someone tried to comfort and encourage her without listening to her hurts or where she was coming from. "When I commented at a Christian women's luncheon that it hurt to think about Mom not being here to see Stephen grow up, the lady next to me jumped in and said, 'Oh, but your mother is with the Lord and I know she is so happy.' I knew that, too, but that didn't mean I didn't miss her and wish she was still sharing our life."

In contrast, some refused to acknowledge there was anything positive in the situation. Linda wanted to tell them about the peace God had given her, but they wouldn't listen. "A couple of Mom's friends were so upset by the accident, that all they wanted to hear was how horribly Dad was doing. Doug tried to say, He's really doing quite well under the circumstances, but they insisted that wasn't true. There was no joy in this tragic loss. Why couldn't they see that although it was painful, God could give peace and joy?"

Resolution

Finally, she realized that dwelling on questions that have no answers wouldn't help her get past the hurt. Instead of asking questions over and over, she began to praise God. "I still have some questions to ask the Lord when I get to heaven, but I knew I had to accept the situation and put my questions to rest."

"Whenever the question of *why* came to me, I'd think, *There is no answer to that.*"

Her faith in Christ has brought her through. "I know that God has allowed this for a purpose. I can't see it now, but someday I will." When she gets negative about her mom's death, she starts praising God. "Even when I don't feel like it, I do it. I know there will be some glory in this and just praise Him in advance."

It took time, however, for Linda to stop worrying about the feelings and thoughts her mother had at the time of the accident. "One afternoon as I prayed, God revealed to me that He never left her, that He was part of her through the whole thing. That gave me a new dimension of God, knowing He goes through everything with us. It gave me peace."

Because her mom had been waiting when Stephen was born, when her second child was due, she asked God to "do something, because when I'm rolled out of the delivery room and Mom's not there, it is going to hurt."

A friend from childbirth classes who was in the hospital having her own baby, was in the recovery room with Linda after Jason's birth.

"When my third child, Amy, was born, I prayed the

same thing. As I came out of the delivery room, a very dear friend was standing there to meet me with the same expression of joy that my mom would have had.''

Her greatest support has come from Doug. ''He knew Mom really well.'' Often he shared the same feelings Linda was having. ''We talked about how we felt about Mom and we cried together.

''Someone has said, 'Life is like a tapestry. The bottom is facing earth and the top is heavenward. God sees the beauty of the work he is doing, and the picture as it is completed. All we see are the knots and loops on the back side. When we get to heaven, we can look down on the tapestry and see it all complete and it will be beautiful. It takes faith in Christ to be able to live with the knots down here.' ''

16

The Loss of a Brother

As Vicki walked in the door that Thursday evening, the phone rang. "Are you all alone?" It was her mom calling from West Virginia. She could tell by her tone of voice that something was wrong.

"I've got some bad news." She asked if Vicki wanted to wait until her husband Dwight got home to hear it. Of course she couldn't stand to wait.

"Mother proceeded to tell me that my youngest brother, Samuel, had been in a car accident. His leg, arm, and jawbone were broken, and his face was crushed. He'd been rushed to surgery to remove his spleen and to try to stop the internal bleeding. He was being given a lot of blood, and the doctors were doing everything they could."

Shocked, Vicki tried to gather her thoughts. *This is un-believable,* she kept thinking. *Samuel is only 17 years old.*

He's an outstanding athlete. How can this be? Should she fly home right away or wait and see what happened?

Because she'd left home for college 10 years before, married Dwight right after graduation, and lived hundreds of miles away for years, going home only for occasional holidays, she'd missed most of Samuel's growing up years. He was only seven when she left for college.

Whenever they did go home, she and Dwight spent a lot of time with him. Interested in learning how to fix things, Samuel had bought one of Dwight's old motorcycles and they worked on it together. Dwight became a role model for Samuel, who decided that after he finished high school the following year, he'd join the Air Force and become a pilot like his brother-in-law who was in training with Mission Aviation Fellowship. Samuel had already talked with a recruiter.

When Dwight got home, the couple talked, prayed, talked some more, and agreed to wait until morning to decide whether to fly to Samuel.

Trying to sleep that night was nearly impossible. When morning came, they decided to go to work and wait to hear from Vicki's mom. Vicki called her church's prayer chain and one at Mission Aviation Fellowship. "What a comfort it was to know that the prayers of so many were being heard by our Father." Mid-morning, her mother called to report that Samuel had spent a long time in surgery and had lost a lot more blood. The doctors felt they'd stopped most of the bleeding, but they couldn't stop it all. Samuel's injuries were so extensive they could offer little hope. His condition had stabilized, but they weren't going to set the broken bones until they stopped the bleeding.

"Since we were in missionary training, Mom and Dad

were worried about the expenses involved in our flying from California to West Virginia and didn't know if we needed to." Vicki told them she and Dwight would wait until evening to decide.

Doctors had told her parents to go home and try to get some rest. They'd barely gotten cleaned up when the hospital called. "You'd better come back. Samuel's blood pressure has dropped and his condition is critical."

Vicki's sisters called her. "We're going to lose him. If you want to see him, you'd better come home. Please come home!"

"Dwight and I got a flight out at midnight on Friday and arrived home Saturday morning.

"Dwight and I went to Intensive Care to see Samuel. I wouldn't have known who he was if the nurse hadn't pointed him out to me. His head was enlarged and the rest of his body was bruised and swollen from all the injuries. He had tubes connected everywhere. I was uncomfortable being with him and didn't know what to say.

"When the nurse said I could talk to him and he could probably hear me, I said, 'Samuel, this is Vicki, I love you. I came to be with you.' That was all I could say. My sister and other brother could come in and just sit and talk to him as if nothing was wrong."

Her biggest concern was that he'd been so athletic. *How unhappy he'd be to be paralyzed!* The Lord was able to heal him, but that didn't seem likely to her. "We were almost ready to pray, 'Lord, take him.' "

Disconnect?

Saturday evening as Vicki's dad talked with Samuel, one of the nurses said, "Mr. Wright, he's already with

Jesus." Although his heart was still beating and they had him on a respirator, there was no brain activity. He'd been given a total of 50 units of blood, but nothing seemed to help. "My parents couldn't say, 'Disconnect him from the life support system.' They decided just to wait." He had a strong heart, and it kept pumping blood when everything else had stopped.

Samuel died on Monday evening.

What Happened at the Hospital

The four days that Vicki's parents spent non-stop at the hospital were very draining. Since it was a 90-minute drive from home, they couldn't return for a short rest. There seemed to be nowhere the family could go to have privacy.

"Every time a nurse would find a place we could be together, another staff member would come and ask us to leave, telling us they needed to use the room. One evening we were told we could rest in the chapel. But before long, the chaplain arrived and asked us to leave."

People seemed so concerned about what to say that they were uncomfortable visiting the family at the hospital. "Usually, the best thing was to put their arm around us and not say anything. We didn't need advice, words of wisdom, or rays of false hope, we needed companions. The hours went by so slowly."

Providing Laughter

A couple of Vicki's parents' friends came, talked quietly, and prayed with the family, sharing their pain. Then they found things that we could laugh about together. "Standing in the main lobby in the middle of the night, one man shared funny experiences that had happened to him, and we all laughed. I think you could hear my dad giggling all the way down the hall. That was such a good break. You can only cry and mourn so much and then there has to be some kind of release. My husband commented on how important that had been.''

The days seemed to follow that pattern. Doctors would tell the family what they were going to try next and what the chances were. There were a lot of tears, but inevitably something occurred that would make them laugh—even something as simple as the terrible food or somebody's funny-looking shoes.

Fruit

One verse Vicki's dad kept quoting was John 12:24. ''Unless a kernel of wheat falls to the ground and dies, it remains only a single seed. But if it dies, it produces many seeds'' (NIV). That came true when several of Samuel's friends came to know the Lord that weekend.

''In the midst of all our darkness was the sparkle of new lives in Christ! That certainly didn't take away our feeling of loss or even make it worthwhile, but it was one ray of 'Sonshine.' Because their own parents weren't able to comfort them we found ourselves ministering to Samuel's friends.''

A Brother's Needs

Vicki's other brother, Andy, who was 22 when Samuel died, took his death very hard. When his folks decided to have a closed casket and use pictures of Samuel on the altar, they asked Andy to select them. Sorting and choosing pictures he wanted to depict

Samuel's life allowed Andy to participate in funeral plans. Although Andy was very quiet about his feelings, he was deeply concerned about where his brother would be buried. One choice was a poorly-kept country cemetery. Andy didn't want his brother buried there. He wanted him in a well-developed and maintained cemetery, even though it was more expensive.

"I could see how important this was and told Andy I'd help cover the cost if Mom and Dad were hesitant to bury him there. Our parents sensed that this was significant and told Andy they'd bury Samuel wherever he preferred. I wouldn't have guessed that would have mattered to him, and was so glad he told me how he felt."

A Special Touch

The other passenger in the car, Samuel's good friend with whom he'd played all kinds of sports, was not injured. The friend had a dried-flowers arrangement made in Samuel's baseball glove for the funeral. It became one of his mother's special keepsakes.

During the week following Samuel's death, the family was surrounded by loving friends.

Unusual Help

People from church organized blood donations to replace that which had been used for Samuel. Over 50 units were given in Samuel's memory.

In some ways, Samuel's friends have helped more than anyone else, his mother says. She received over a dozen letters from them in which they told what he meant to them, how much he loved his parents, and that he always wanted to please them. His friends have stayed in touch and continue to check on her.

"Mom and Dad have welcomed Samuel's friends and have been touched by their genuine interest. They couldn't ask for a better testimonial than to have their son's peers share what an exceptional person he was."

The same week that Samuel's accident took place, a young attorney from the same small town, who had recently begun a practice, was killed in an auto accident. His parents, who owned a local restaurant, called several times, sent flowers and catered a complete meal. "We asked them how they could possibly do these things for us. They told me, 'The way we receive comfort is by comforting someone else.' "

Samuel's family wanted to talk about him and hear about special times others had enjoyed with him. "His life had ended, but our love for him had not."

Vicki says she appreciated the cards and letters she received from former school mates. "They were so thoughtful to make a special effort to locate me and offer their love."

Memory Fades

"Supporters quickly dwindled just about the time we really needed them," Vicki remembers. "Mom spent hour after hour in her room, lonely, crying, and asking 'Why?' She needed friends to stay in touch and initiate outside activities. It was several months before she wanted to do things on her own."

Misguided Callers

Unfortunately, the family received many phone calls from people telling them of others who'd been killed in car accidents or sons who had died. "Although they were probably attempting to let us know we weren't the only family to face this kind of loss, that was not what we needed to hear," Vicki says. "What we needed was for them to tell us they were praying for us, knew what we were going through and were available to help. Hearing third and fourth hand that someone else had faced a tragedy, doesn't take the loss away."

Helping Children

Especially upset by his death was Samuel's seven-year-old nephew. When it was explained that Samuel had been in great pain, but that he was with Jesus now and much happier, Jason responded, "Well then, I wish I could die, so I could see Uncle Sam."

Months after his uncle's death, Jason occasionally asked, "If Uncle Sam is really better off in heaven, why can't I go and be with him?" That taught Vicki how important it is to be honest with children, and also to be careful about their concept of death. "It's been hard for the kids to see such a change in their Grandma. Most of the time she's just the same, but she does have mood swings and they can't understand why she is so upset."

Grieving Continues

There are constant reminders of the family's loss. For his mother it is the empty house and the lack of activity that surrounded Samuel's life. Back-to-school ads remind her that she doesn't have a son to ready for school. Every high school sports article brings back Samuel's athletic participation. During June he would have completed his senior year, every graduation function she heard about upset her.

Samuel's birthday is also the day her niece was born, so that's a day of conflicting emotions. It's filled with the excitement of a toddler's birthday party and also moments of heartache. The impact of his death continues as his absence is felt in many different areas.

When Vicki returned home to California and friends greeted her with, "Hi. How are you?" she didn't know if they knew about Samuel's death or were just offering a casual salutation.

"If they did know, it would have been helpful if they'd said, 'Hi, Vicki. I've been praying for you. How've you been doing since you got home?' or 'I heard about Samuel's death. I'm so sorry. Was it difficult for you to leave your family?' I needed them to identify that they knew what I had been through and initiate the conversation about him. Otherwise, I just responded, 'I'm fine.'

"Samuel's loss still hurts. I still wonder why this had to happen. What bothers me most, though, is that I'd lived away from home for almost 10 years and really didn't know him well.

"I only have one brother left, and I don't really know him either. I have committed myself to spend more time with him. I want to be his friend as well as his sister."

17

The Forgotten Griever

Look, There's the Child's Father

Look—over there in the corner.
There's the child's father.
Don't shut him out.
Don't pass him by.
He's grieving, too.
Support him.
Understand him.
Love him, too.
Look—over there in the corner.
There's the child's father.
Be with him as he mourns.

Gladys Chmiel

As comforters, we need to be aware that more

people are affected by a crisis or loss than the immediate family. But often, these others are forgotten or ignored. When I saw Vicki after her brother Samuel died, she told me how that happened in her family.

"My husband Dwight was probably closer to my brother Samuel than anyone else. While Samuel was in the hospital, Dwight was with him more than anyone. Even though Samuel was unconscious, he'd stand with him and hold his hand.

"Dwight told me that everyone came up to him and asked, 'How's Vicki? How's her family?' No one ever asked him how he was taking it. No one took into consideration that he was hurting, too. Dwight said, 'Nobody was asking about me because I am just an in-law.' "

As Vicki said those words, I realized that I'd done exactly the same thing. At church when Vicki was absent from service, I went over to Dwight and asked him how she was doing. He told me, 'She just has a bad cold and decided that she should stay home this morning.' I asked him to give her my love and tell her that I was praying for her. Dwight thanked me for my interest and assured me he'd tell Vicki.

Never once did I ask Dwight how he was. In my efforts to be sensitive to Vicki's needs, I had totally overlooked her husband.

Truly, Dwight was a forgotten griever.

A description of some who, like Dwight, may be forgotten grievers and need your loving comfort too, follows.

Children

We may overlook children's emotional needs because we think that they're too young to understand and that they won't grieve. As I recall my childhood, I realize now that I had feelings of loss over my brothers by the time I was six-years-old.

My sister, on the other hand, who was four years younger and had a totally different personality than me, remembers little of the trauma surrounding my brothers' problems.

Children need to talk about their feelings and about the person who died. Encourage them to share what's on their minds. Talk about ways the deceased will be missed.

Pay attention to the children. If they are convinced you'll listen, they'll tell you when they are sad and why. Often they'll lead the way for others to express their grief by creating an open atmosphere in which to share.

Be honest with children. Explain death clearly and truthfully. Use the correct words. Don't say the deceased is asleep when he is really unconscious or dead, otherwise a child may develop a fear of sleeping. Children need to know that the heart has stopped, the dead person doesn't need to eat, and that he isn't breathing any more.

Depending on a child's maturity, he'll need to know what happened to the body. Tell him about heaven and that he'll see his loved ones there. Go through pictures of him with his loved one and talk about special times they shared together, so he'll have positive memories of the deceased. Encourage him to tell you when he's thinking about the one who's gone and talk together about how much you both miss them.

That's what we did with six-year-old Randy, Jr. when Grammy was taken to the hospital. I went to school early to pick him up. As we sat on the grass outside our house, my husband and I explained that Grammy Chapman was taken to the hospital that morning and that she was very sick. We went on to say that she has had a very bad disease in her body, that doctors were taking care of her, but it didn't look like she'd get better. She was unconscious, we explained ("unconscious" was a new word, and we taught him its meaning), and she was probably going to die.

Randy looked up at me. "I'm not sad because we are all going to die sometime."

I asked him if he wanted to go see Grammy even though she wouldn't be able to talk to him. He said, "Not right now, Mom." I told him that Mommy was sad about Grammy and anytime he had any questions I wanted him to tell me and we'd talk about it. He gave me a big hug and we went in the house.

Later that afternoon I called the hospital and the doctor said he didn't expect Grammy to live through the night. I decided to ask Randy again if he'd like to go see Grammy.

"No, I was with her yesterday and we had a good talk!" he told me. He was content with his positive memories of yesterday and didn't feel a need to see her in an unconscious state. He was not left out of anything, yet he was not forced to do something he didn't need to do.

The next afternoon when I received the news that Grammy had died, I called Randy, Jr. into our bedroom and told him. He answered simply, "Well, I guess that means no more elevators for me." (Grammy had been living on the second floor of the retirement home and every time my children visited her they rode up in the elevator.)

But a few days later when I picked up Randy from the babysitter's, he told me, "I was sad today."

"What about?" I asked him.

"That I'm not going to see Grammy anymore." I told

him that I was sad about that too and that it was okay for us to feel that way.

When I brought a box of things home from Grammy's room, Randy, Jr. found some pictures of him that we had sent to her. "I want to put these in my room so that every time I look at them I'll remember Grammy," he told me. Of course, I gave them to him and he put them on top of his dresser. He's talked about them several times since then.

No matter how well we deal with children's grief, their feelings will always be part of them. One parent who miscarried mid-term told me that her 12-year-old daughter came from school complaining that she'd had a terrible day. "The kids picked on me; I couldn't eat my lunch. Everything went wrong!"

"Do you know why this was such a terrible day?" her mom asked.

"Yes, this was the day that Megan was supposed to be born!"

Never underestimate the impact a loss or crisis has had on a child. Their attitudes and concepts about death and tragedy are related not only to their age, but to their maturity and experience as well. The way we deal with children must be highly individualized. On the surface, they may seem to adjust to a crisis easily, but this may be a self-protection. The real task of completing their grieving process may await them later in life. If losses pile up on one another, resolution of a new loss will be more difficult.

When my second brother, Larry, died at 20-years-old, I experienced all the emotion that accompanies a loss. It was much greater than I expected. Soon I realized that I was re-experiencing the loss and accompanying grief from my childhood. Very often, a new loss will bring past feelings to the surface. We need to face our feelings with new maturity and understanding.

Parental mood swings can be frightening to children if they're not discussed. I remember one morning when Mom was in a terrible mood. Everything we did seemed to set her off. I was getting mad at her for being so upset with us when Dad asked me to come into the bedroom.

"Mom is upset today because it is Larry's fifth birthday." It's appropriate for a child to see their parents' sadness, but they need to know the reason for it.

Grandparents

In comforting a family who has lost a child, we often fail to realize that grandparents grieve also. They may not react the same way or to the same extent as the parents, but they do grieve.

Their grief is two-sided. One is for their grandchild who died, and the other is the sadness and pain of seeing their own child in such torment. To see one's child in pain and not be able to ease it leaves them feeling helpless and frustrated.

The death of a grandchild can bring back memories of their own past losses—a painful revival of the grief they thought was over. When my pregnancy ended mid-term and we discovered that my baby had had a severe abnormality, my mom grieved, not only over the loss of her grandchild and my pain, but because it brought back the loss of her own sons.

Husbands and Fathers

When there is a crisis, the expected male role is to be strong. However, men have genuine, deep feelings of grief as well. Often men work through their feelings differently than women, but that doesn't mean they need less concern or support.

Husbands often feel that they must support their families and not disclose how much they're hurting. They may feel that the attention is going to their families and that no one is considering their needs. Husbands and fathers need to know that their friends are praying for them. They need friends to offer them comfort, too.

Others who may be forgotten grievers include:

In-laws. Not seen as part of the immediate family, their feelings are not expected to be as strong as other relatives.

Close friends. Because of the intimacy of their relationship, their response to a loss could be even greater than that of the family.

Siblings. Most attention is focused on the parents' need at the time of tragedy, but a brother or sister may be hurting very deeply as well.

Grandchildren. Because of their special relationship, grandchildren have their own individual needs during a crisis involving their grandparents.

Be sensitive to all the people affected by a crisis and God will be able to use you to minister to the forgotten grievers.

A Crisis Checklist

DO

Respond in a timely manner with a card, a call, or a visit.

DON'T

Don't wait a long time before you make your initial contact.

DO

Offer simple, understanding statements such as: "I feel for you during this difficult time." "This must be very hard for you." "I share your feelings of loss." "I wish I could take the hurt away." Comments like these let the person know you acknowledge their pain and it's okay for them to feel that way.

DON'T

Don't try to minimize their pain with comments like, "It's probably for the best." "Things could be worse." "You'll remarry." "You're young, you can always have another one." "You're strong, you'll get over it soon." "You know God is in control." Comments like these might be an attempt to offer hope, but to a hurting person, they sound as though you don't comprehend the enormity of what's happened.

DO

Say "I'm so sorry." Then add, "I know how special he was to you." "I'll miss her also." "I want to help you; I'm available anytime you need me." "I've been praying for you. Is there something specific I should be praying for?"

DON'T

Don't say "I'm so sorry," and end the sentence. Your hurting friend is probably sorry, too, but he can't respond to that kind of comment.

DO

Be aggressive with your willingness to help. Ask yourself, "What would I need if I were in a similar situation?" Offer specific things you can do for them, like, "I'm on my way to the store. What can I pick up for you?" "Would tomorrow be a good day to help you with the laundry?" "Would the children like to come over and play this afternoon?" Most of the time, a person in a crisis can't decide what he does need. Besides, he probably doesn't want to impose.

DON'T

Don't just say, "Is there anything I can do to help?"

DO

Encourage them to keep a journal or write down their thoughts and feelings. Often, just seeing their thoughts on paper helps them deal with what they are facing.

DON'T

Don't say, "You shouldn't feel that way."

DO

Agree when the individual expresses their feelings. Say, "Yes, what happened to you isn't fair and doesn't make any sense," whether or not you share the same perspective.

DON'T

Don't offer spiritual answers as to why they're facing this problem or tell them that they'll be a stronger person afterwards. We don't know why tragedies happen—why certain people have to go through such trauma. We do our friends a disservice by offering possible explanations.

DO

Allow them all the time they need to deal effectively with all the phases of their grief.

DON'T

Don't put time tables on your hurting friend's recovery. Your inference that they're not coping well or should be their old self by now, only hinders their progress.

DO

Give spiritual encouragement from your heart, and include Bible verses that have comforted you at a difficult time.

DON'T

Don't quote Bible verses as a way to correct or minimize their feelings. Think very carefully, asking yourself if a passage will communicate comfort or condemnation. Never offer spiritual suggestions from a position of superiority or self-righteousness.

DO

Carefully consider what you can and would like to do. Be creative. Use your gifts and talents to help. Your willing spirit and creative efforts will minister to your hurting friend.

Don't put yourself under pressure to perform tasks that you really don't want to do.

DO

Be honest about your experiences. If you haven't endured their particular kind of tragedy, say "I haven't been through what you're facing, but I want you to know I care about you and will support you through the difficult time ahead." If you've had a similar crisis, tell them about it briefly, adding that you can empathize with their feelings. Of course, you can't completely understand because you haven't been through the past experiences that laid the foundation 'or their reaction.

DON'T

Don't say "I understand" when you haven't faced the same situation. Telling someone that everything will be all right when you have never known the depth of their hardship, is an empty statement. And they don't need to hear horror stories of people you know who've been through something similar.

DO

Continue keeping in touch, letting them know you're praying for them. Ask how they're *really* doing and send thoughtful notes with encouraging words.

DON'T

Don't ignore their needs after the immediate crisis has subsided.

DO

Realize that their hearts are full of pain and turmoil. Let them know that you will listen to their feelings and want to be part of that pain.

DON'T

Don't expect unrealistic optimism or levity from your hurting person.

DO

Indicate your love by saying, "I really feel awkward because I'm not sure what to say, what you need, or how to help you, but I want you to know that I love you. I'm praying for you and I'm available."

DON'T

Don't offer cliches or be vainly optimistic to cover up your insecurities.

DO

Allow the individual to make the decisions and take the necessary steps to deal with the trauma. No one can tell another what to feel or not to feel.

DON'T

Don't use "should's" or "if only's" such as: "You should give the clothes away." "You should go back to work and get over this." "You should have more faith." "If only you had watched him more carefully." "If only you hadn't been so strict." "If only you ate better."

154

DO

Respond cautiously and prayerfully with uplifting and edifying ideas when your friends ask for your help in their tragedy.

DON'T

Don't offer unasked-for advice. If they weren't solicited, your suggestions may not be appreciated.

DO

Provide long-term, unconditional support. Let them know that everyone deals with trauma in a different way. You have no expectation of how much time it should take or how they should behave. Assure them that whatever it takes, you'll be there with them through it.

DON'T

Don't be critical or judgmental. Don't say things like "This wouldn't have happened if . . ." "There must be sin in your life." "You're not trusting God with your feelings."

18

Be There!

Pain cannot and should not be removed
from the long arduous trail of mourning, but
it can be endured better when understanding
spouses, relatives, friends and professionals
travel along with the hurting.

When Pregnancy Fails[4]
by Susan Borg and Judith Lasker

When I asked my uncle, Col. James Chapman, what
he'd learned about comforting in his 30 years as an Air
Force chaplain, he thought briefly and shared this
experience.

"The most valuable lesson I learned happened just
a few months after I'd been ordained. I was in my
twenties and assigned to Amarillo Air Force Base in
Texas. Outside the base was a ramshackled community

where the residents lived in old World War II temporary housing. A couple worked as caretakers. The husband was a handyman and his wife looked after the area.

"One night another chaplain called me. 'Get the police. There's been a murder in Cammes Village.' I'd never handled a murder before, and drove out to the village not knowing what I'd do or say.

"When I arrived, I found that the son of this couple had brutally murdered his fiancee. Too stunned to do anything significant or dramatic, I stood by while the police handled details and the body was removed. I moved a few things, made some phone calls, and tried to calm the mother.

"When I left at midnight, I didn't think I'd been very helpful or comforting. I felt guilty that I'd not known what to do, so I continued visiting this family as the weeks went on. Whenever I could, I'd drop in and say hello.

"As time passed, the son came to trial. It seemed inevitable that he'd be convicted of murder. I planned to sit with the family at the trial. But one day I received a phone call informing me that the son had killed himself. Although I knew I needed to be with the family, once again I felt totally inadequate to meet their needs. What could I say? What could I do?

"I spent time with the parents, listened to their thoughts and fears, and offered them my compassion.

"In the months that followed, I kept going to see the family, just sitting and visiting with them and letting them talk.

"One day, the father looked up and told me, 'Chaplain, we want to thank you for the time you've spent with us and all that you've done for us. I don't know how we'd have made it through all this if it hadn't been for you.'

"I didn't know I'd done anything that was either right or helpful. All I knew was that I kept going to see them. I was willing to sit with them and be part of their grief.

"This taught me very early in my ministerial career that it's not important to have big speeches prepared or to do major things, but rather *to be there.*"

I learned a similar lesson when I accompanied a friend to a difficult doctor's appointment one day. "I wish I'd had time to put on a different dress," I told her.

"Lauren, you could have worn your bathing suit and I wouldn't have cared. All that matters is that you are here." What she needed at that moment wasn't well-thought-out words of wisdom or beautiful clothing. She needed my presence.

Each person I talk with who has had a recent loss says, "The thing I needed most during my difficult time was people coming by and calling me to see what they could do and what I might need." Yet, so few want to visit those who hurt. Many rationalize that since they might say the wrong thing, it's better not to go.

It's easy to pray that God will comfort someone, but it takes effort and genuine concern to be the one God uses as a comforter. I was in a Bible study a few years ago when a member's husband died. The whole group prayed sincerely for her and asked the Lord to comfort her.

The leader asked if I would be willing to give some suggestions of things they could do for her. As I opened my mouth to speak, he started on with the lesson. No one ever mentioned it again.

The following week when they asked one another if anyone knew how Marge was doing, it became apparent that not one had even called her.

The most important thing you can do for someone is not to speak flowery words or perform marvelous deeds. Just give them your continued support. The most important thing you can do is *to be there*.

Acknowledge that your friend is hurting.

Support them while they grieve normally and appropriately.

Help them come to a healthy resolution of their trauma.

Never minimize their loss or try to diminish the feelings they are having. As we allow them to share their emotions openly and honestly, we'll help them conclude their grieving naturally.

Take time to meditate on God's words in Isaiah 40:1, "Comfort, comfort ye my people." The effort you put into your hurting person's life will make a difference. With your loving, non-judgmental, unconditional support, you can make the path a little easier and the load a little lighter for your friend. God will bless you for all the special efforts you make on behalf of your hurting person and will, in turn, make you a blessing to them.

There may be times when, despite all your sincerity, empathy, and sensitivity, no words seem appropriate. The best thing you can do is to give your hurting person a strong hug and admit, "I don't know what to say."

Appendix

How to Form a Support Group

Take Me Back

Take me back where I belong,
Let me once again be strong.
Let me help my friends in need,
With a kind word or act or deed.

So much sorrow has filled my life,
I know I've been neglecting others' strife.
I still have been with them in thought and
   prayer,
I love them so much and I really do care.

But they need more from me—I know they do,

161

Take me back so I can once more help them
through.

Gladys Chmiel

As a hurting person begins to emerge from the depths
of his grief, he'll see that there is a tiny light at the end
of his long, dark tunnel. Gradually, he comes to a
healthy resolution. Resolving the grief process does not
mean that the sense of loss or trauma has gone away,
but it does indicate an acceptance and desire to continue with a full and meaningful life.

Those who've made it through the forest can go back
and guide others through and offer them the same
comfort with which they were comforted. One of the
ways to do that is through a support group.

The following is a letter I wrote to a mother whose
teenaged son was killed in a tragic car accident. She
asked me what a support group was and how she could
get one started.

Dear Mrs. Wright,

Thank you so much for your letter requesting information about starting a support group for bereaved
parents in your area. Since I have been instrumental
in forming support groups here in Southern California
and have just returned from a parent support group conference, I feel I'll be able to offer you the guidance
necessary to start one.

I'm confident you'll find this a rewarding experience
as well as one that helps you come to a healthy resolution of your own loss. I know that a support group can
never replace the son you lost, but as you see other
parents' lives touched as a result of your efforts, you'll
sense a feeling of fulfillment. By comforting and
supporting other parents, you'll not only lift them up

but acquire new understanding and acceptance of your situation.

Before you can begin a support group you'll need to understand:

1. What a support group should be.
2. Why there is a need for forming a support group.
3. Who the people are you should be reaching with your group.
4. How to begin such a group.

What is a Support Group?

A support group is a gathering of individuals who've had a common experience, want to share their own needs and offer understanding and compassion to other participants who have similar needs. A group can be a way of coping with the complexities of a particular experience which no one else seems to understand. It provides a place to work through the trauma with others who are learning to do the same thing. Members serve as role models to newer ones. They are examples, because they have survived. It has hurt and been difficult, but you do make it through.

I was introduced to many types of support groups at a conference I attended. Although each was different, they all had in common the fact that they reached out to people in similar situations and worked to encourage one another in their difficult times.

Kinds of support groups included parents of children with cancer, or with a specific disability, parents who've had children in neonatal intensive care units, parents who've had a pregnancy loss or stillbirth, and parents who have lost a child at any age. They also included widows, divorcees, and people with a family member facing a fatal disease. The list goes on and on.

A support group must offer emotional support to its members as well as provide an open atmosphere where they can safely vocalize their hurts, frustrations, and disappointments without the fear of judgment. It provides a time to meet others who've been in the same place; an opportunity to find sympathetic friends.

Helping someone else through a difficult situation helps us put our own traumas in perspective. Giving this kind of support makes one feel useful and helps one see some positive aspect to the hard times he's experienced.

The function of such a group is not to provide intensive therapy, but rather to offer an atmosphere where feelings can be expressed and will be understood. This creates a feeling of acceptance and allows people to share what's on their heart, or simply to observe if they wish.

Why is There a Need for Support Groups?

Most parents I come in contact with say, "No one seems to understand what I'm going through" or "Why am I having such a hard time dealing with this loss?" A person can best be helped by someone who has been there—someone who has experienced a similar trauma and has successfully dealt with his experience. They share a common condition and are able to help each other cope. Many join a support group to get help themselves, but end up ministering to others.

One of the most important reasons to participate in a support group is that those outside may be tired of listening to the bereaved's problems, to the rehashing of their experiences, and feel that the mourning period should be over. It's this very time that they need a sympathetic ear.

Many people have asked me, "Why isn't it enough just to go to a Bible study and church to find help in overcoming one's grief?" Unfortunately, the average Bible study, care group, or fellowship isn't able to minister to the specific emotional needs of someone facing a personal trauma.

Comments like "Just put the whole thing behind you and get on with your life" or "If you just had enough faith you wouldn't need any other help" serve to illustrate why there is such a need for support groups. People have no concept of the depth or the significance of someone's personal trauma unless they themselves have already faced a similar situation.

How Does a Support Group Get Started?

All it takes to start a support group is one person who has had to face a difficult situation and realizes that there is a need to form a group. Ours began with three of us who lost our babies midpregnancy. To protect our confidentiality in our medical records, a professional advisor contacted each person to see if she was interested in belonging to the group. Groups formed from the lay community do not need to be concerned with that complication.

At our first meeting, held at my house, we began by introducing ourselves and sharing a little about our loss. Conversation flowed quite easily because we were learning that we were not alone—that someone else had the same reactions and feelings. It became very clear to us that we shared emotions and experiences unique to our situation and people who hadn't faced this didn't understand what we were going through. Instead of seeing ourselves as strange, it became plain that our reactions were probably quite normal.

When that first meeting concluded, we realized that we had a common bond and because of what we'd experienced, we could help others facing the same loss. Certainly, we needed each other for support and to help comfort others. Never could we take away the impact of the loss, but we might help make it a little more bearable.

Meetings were set for the third Wednesday of each month at 1:30 P.M. Since our group consisted of mothers, a daytime meeting seemed to be the most appropriate. There may be other kinds of groups that are geared towards husbands as well, and an evening meeting would be better. That's a decision each group needs to decide for itself.

Our first few meetings were very informal and mainly a time to get acquainted, share our difficulties, and tell how we dealt with them. As time went by, we felt the group needed some structure as well as a plan for welcoming new people.

We decided that the first half hour would be devoted to socializing. Then our meeting would proceed around a certain topic. Sometimes, a guest speaker such as a clergyman, medical professional, or parent who is experienced in an area in which we were interested, would be invited to speak.

When we do not have a speaker (which is probably less than half the time), a group member is responsible for the topic and discussion time. By having a planned topic or speaker, the meeting has some form, but we still leave time for the sharing that needs to take place.

Our meetings generally last from one and one-half to two hours. Simple refreshments are made available. Somehow, a cup of coffee or glass of juice in our hands makes us a little more comfortable. Most of the women come with specific needs and burdens on their hearts, but it takes time before they feel comfortable to talk about them.

Most of the names for new members are referrals from local physicians and hospitals. Other ways to get them include local newspaper advertisements, word of mouth, or notices in activity centers such as the YWCA or Women's Club.

When we get a referral, we try to match that person to one of our members with similar qualities such as age and kind of loss. Unless the parent prefers to call us, the member usually makes the first contact. Generally, they talk on the phone several times, get together for lunch or a casual visit and share their similar experiences. Quite a bit of peer counseling goes on.

Once they've established a personal relationship, the new parent is invited to join us for one of our monthly meetings. Usually it's best the sponsoring member accompanies the new parent to the first meeting.

One mother told me she'd come if she could just listen and didn't have to say anything.

"Would it be all right if I introduced you and shared a little about your experience?"

She agreed. By the end of the meeting, she was adding comments freely. No matter how loving the atmosphere is, a group encounter is usually a threatening situation. No one should ever be pushed to open up or discuss something she's not ready to share.

Whenever a new member comes to a meeting, we introduce ourselves and share a little about our loss. Although we don't want to belabor our problems, we do want to show that we are experiencing similar feelings. If the new parent doesn't feel comfortable speaking for herself, her sponsor member will introduce her and give a little background information.

Our role as a support group is threefold.

First, to comfort a new parent facing a loss on a one-to-one basis as well as in a group setting.

Second, to provide a support system for those who are ministering to new members.

Third, to help make medical professionals aware of our needs and how they can better handle us at the time of our loss.

We've prepared a panel discussion we've delivered to nurses and physicians in many Southern California hospitals. Changes in understanding and care for parents who have lost a pregnancy midterm have taken place.

A mother I'd worked with called me in tears one evening. "No one understands me!" she poured out. "They try to comfort me, but they don't know how I feel. I told them I just had to talk to Lauren. She was the only one who did."

I listened while she told me about how cheated she felt and how angry she was that her baby had died. "It's okay to feel that way," I assured her.

I felt that all my efforts had been worthwhile. We'd developed a relationship and she knew she could call me any time and I'd share her pain. I was so thankful I was there to listen.

A support group can function very well as a ministry of a specific church. However, I encourage you to think of your support group as a ministry not associated with a church.

Ours doesn't have a sponsor and operates independently. Referrals come from the medical community. Parents of many different faiths attend that I feel wouldn't have come if the group were associated with one particular church. I've been able to make an impact on lives that wouldn't have happened otherwise.

It's not necessary to have reached a complete resolution of your own loss in order to minister effectively to other parents in the same situation. You'll be a comfort to them and at the same time they'll be a support system for you. A person doesn't need total victory to be able to help someone else. They only need to have faced the same situation and to have made it one step farther. Then they can reach back and help carry the other person along.

I know you'll find this effort a very rewarding experience. In our group we've found an atmosphere of acceptance and encouragement that has greatly helped to ease the pain. All of us are very sensitive to the needs of other persons facing similar situations.

Something *can* be done to help. We can never make the experience easy or satisfying, but we can help make it a little less devastating. May God richly bless your efforts as you comfort others in a way that only you can do.

With Compassion,

Lauren L. Briggs

NOTES

1. Bertha G. Simos, *A Time to Grieve* (Family Service Association of America, 1979), p. 1.
2. Ibid., p. 19.
3. Susan Borg and Judith Lasker, *When Pregnancy Fails* (Beacon Press, 1981), p. 20.
4. Ibid., foreword.